THE
JEWISH-AMERICAN
HERITAGE

THE
JEWISH-AMERICAN
HERITAGE

David M. Brownstone

Part of the America's Ethnic Heritage series
General Editors: David M. Brownstone and Irene M. Franck

Facts On File Publications
New York, New York ● Oxford, England

The Jewish-American Heritage

Library of Congress Cataloging-in-Publication Data

Brownstone, David M.
  The Jewish heritage.

  (America's ethnic heritage)
  Bibliography: p.
  Includes index.
  Summary: Explores the history, culture, and contribu-
tions of Jews in America from the arrival of the earliest
European settlers to the present day.
    1. Jews—United States—History—Juvenile literature.
  2. Judaism—United States—History—Juvenile literature.
  3. United States—Ethnic relations—Juvenile literature.
  [1. Jews—United States—History. 2. Judaism.
  3. United States— Ethnic relations] I. Title.
  II. Series.
  E184.J5B744   1988   973'.04924   87-19905
  ISBN 0-8160-1628-3

Series Design: Cathy Rincon

Printed in the United States of America

10 9 8 7 6 5 4 3 2 1

Contents

Preface

The Jewish-American Heritage is a volume in the *America's Ethnic Heritage* series, which explores the unique background of each of America's ethnic groups—their history and culture, their reasons for leaving home, their long journey to America, their waves of settlement in the new land, their often-difficult years of adjustment as they made their way into the American mainstream, and their contributions to the overall society we call "America."

We would like to thank the many people who helped us in completing this work: our expert typists, Shirley Fenn and Mary Racette; Domenico Firmani, photo researcher *par excellence*; skilled cartographer Mark Stein; James Warren, our excellent editor at Facts On File; his very able assistant, Claire Johnston; publisher Edward Knappman, who supported this series from the start; and the many fine members of the Facts On File editorial and production staff.

We also express our special appreciation to the many librarians whose help has been indispensable in completing this work, especially to the incomparable staff of the Chappaqua Library—director Mark Hasskarl; the reference staff, including Mary Platt, Paula Peyraud, Terry Cullen, Martha Alcott, Carolyn Jones, and, formerly, Helen Barolini and Karen Baker; Jane McKean and Marcia Van Fleet and the whole circulation staff—and the many other librarians who, through the Interlibrary Loan network, have provided us with the research tools so vital to our work.

David M. Brownstone
Irene M. Franck

America's Ethnic Heritage

The United States is a great sea of peoples. All the races, nations, and beliefs of the world are met here. We live together, joined with each other while at the same time keeping our own separate identities. And it works. Sometimes there is pain and struggle for equality and justice, but it works—and will for as long as we all want it to.

We have brought with us to America all the ethnic heritages of the world. In that respect, there is no other place like this on Earth, no other place where all the histories of all the peoples come together. Some have therefore called the United States a great "melting pot." But that is not quite right. We do not mix and completely merge our ethnic heritages. Instead we mix them, partially merge them, and at the same time keep important parts of them whole. The result is something unique called an American.

1

The Jewish Heritage

This book is about the history of American Jews. It is about who they were; why and how they came to America; where they came from and where they settled; how they lived and grew in communities within the larger American community; and how they helped shape and were shaped by their new country. Putting it a little differently, this book is about that combination of history, qualities, skills, accomplishments, and hopes that all together make up the Jewish-American heritage.

To begin to see all that fairly clearly, you have to go back a long time—in fact, thousands of years. The Jews are relatively few in number, but their ideas have had a powerful influence on the shape of the world since long before the time of Christ. From very early times, the Jews have been the People of the Book, that book being the Hebrew Bible, which is Christianity's Old Testament. Jewish religious beliefs have been basic building blocks for three of the world's great religions—Judaism, Christianity, and Mohammedanism. That alone makes the Jews one of the world's important historical peoples.

But there is much more to the Jewish heritage. Some special qualities and skills have been developed in the thousands of years of Jewish history. Much of that history, especially in Europe, where most of America'a Jews came from, has been a story of oppression—and great responding strength on the part of the Jews. So we must explore the story of that oppression and the kind of strong people that resulted from it if we are to see the Jewish heritage clearly.

In trying to understand the Jewish-American heritage, then, we have to first understand a good deal about the older Jewish heritage, and about the lives Jews led before they came to America.

The Three Waves of Jewish Immigrants

Three waves of Jewish immigrants came from Europe into what was first colonial America and then the United States. Each wave was about 10 times as large as the next. Each wave will be discussed in detail further on in this book, but it is worthwhile to get a bird's-eye view right at the start.

The first wave was composed mostly of Jews from Spain and Portugal, and came during the century and a half between the 1630's and the American Revolution in 1776. Many of these Jews did not come from Spain and Portugal directly. Rather, they came by way of Brazil, Holland, and England, all countries to which Jews had fled after they were expelled from Spain in 1492 and Portugal in 1497.

Some Jews during colonial times also came from central and eastern Europe, mostly from Germany and Poland, and usually through England first. These, along with the Spanish and Portuguese Jews, were the first wave of American Jewish immigrants. Their numbers were small, and there were only a few thousand Jews altogether in the new United States just after the Revolution. But their small communities are an important part of the story of the growth of the Jewish-American heritage, for they made real contributions to the life and thought of their times, and to the story of the American Revolution.

The second wave of Jewish immigrants was mostly from Germany and other German-speaking European countries, with relatively few from other parts of Europe. This was a much larger group, numbering about 250,000-300,000 in all, and arriving from the 1830s through the early 1880s. These German Jews formed a large national community and were at the same time part of the much larger German immigration and of the growing German-American community of those years. German Jews played important roles in the settlement of the American West, during the Civil War, and as industrial America began to develop after the war. After the 1880s some Jews continued to come from Germany but not very many, compared to the number that were, by then, coming from Eastern Europe.

The third wave of Jewish immigrants was mostly from Russia and Eastern Europe, and arrived in flight from intolerable oppression. This was a huge immigration, numbering about 2,500,000 in all and arriving

Whether young or old, like this grandmother at Ellis Island in 1926, Jews brought with them to America a love of freedom and a deep store of hope and determination. (Photo by Lewis W. Hine, New York Public Library)

between the early 1880s and the mid-1920s. It was reduced to a trickle in the mid-1920s, as was all immigration from eastern and southern Europe, because the U.S. Congress passed very restrictive immigration laws in the early 1920s, making further mass immigration from those areas impossible. This wave of Jewish immigrants eventually mixed and partially merged with the German-speaking and Spanish-Portuguese Jews who had come before. Together they formed that part of the population of the country that is the Jewish ethnic group and shares the Jewish-American heritage. In recent years, some additional tens of thousands of Russian Jews and small numbers of Israeli Jews have also become Jewish-Americans.

We speak of the Jewish-American ethnic group here and throughout this book. Most of the people in this group are also Jews by religious belief, adhering to the Reform, Conservative, Orthodox, or one of the ultra-Orthodox, versions of Judaism. But very many Jewish-Americans identify themselves as Jews and yet are not religious at all. If people consider themselves Jews, they are for the purposes of this book considered to be part of the Jewish-American ethnic group. Note also that, because of the way Jewish history has developed, many Jews consider themselves Jews and also part of other ethnic groups, as when someone is a Canadian-Jewish-American or a German-Jewish-American. In the United States, the same people can and do share many ethnic heritages at once, whether in the first immigrant generation or later on, when you may trace a dozen different ethnic heritages in a single family.

The Heritage

What heritage, then, have Jews brought to America out of thousands of years of history, from many lands and from many different kinds of situations?

First, a thirst for freedom. All the wrongs and hurts of a thousand years of European Jewish history have only served to strengthen that thirst. The first Spanish-Portuguese Jews came to North America as refugees, to New Amsterdam (now New York) in 1634. The German Jews, too, came seeking freedom in the 19th century. The Eastern European Jews came in flight, seeking the freedom they lived to find and help grow in the United States. The Russian Jews come today to find far more freedom than the

Soviet Union has to offer.

Next, strength—personal strength and the strength of communities used to surviving and growing in difficult conditions. This is not just the strength of a rock, which may shatter when hit hard enough. The strength that the Jews bring is rocklike when it must be, but flexible enough to be able to adapt to new conditions.

Pride, too. It takes pride, and a great deal of it, to keep your family and community going while being persecuted just because you are a Jew—and that is one of the main facts of a thousand years of European Jewish history. Much has been written about how strange it was that so many Jews allowed themselves to be led unresisting to Hitler's gas chambers. Jews all over Europe resisted the Nazis, fighting them in the streets, fields, mountains, and forests, fighting them even when the odds were hopeless, as in the Warsaw Ghetto. That took rocklike strength, and enormous pride and courage.

Also the ability to hope, which Jews share with all those who came to America. Those who pioneer must also be able to hope, and Jews have demonstrated that ability in situation after situation, as they have moved about Europe and the world in search of a better life for themselves and their children.

What else? A strong feeling for family and community, which was so important for survival in Europe. It was to prove tremendously useful in the New World, as well.

Jews also brought skills and talents that would prove to be of great value to their new country. Jews had been some of the greatest scholars of the ancient world and continued to be great scholars and thinkers as the European world developed for two thousand years after the birth of Christ. Jews are the people of the Old Testament, and early Christians who had been born Jews had much to do with the creation of the New Testament. From ancient times, in all the lands around the Mediterranean Sea, Jews worked as scientists, physicians, philosophers, translators, mapmakers, and teachers, and as leaders in these and every other branch of human knowledge. This is a major part of the heritage that Jews bring to America and to the whole world.

Jews, like Greeks and Armenians, were also some of the greatest traders and merchants of the ancient world. They carried those skills with them into the European world. In Europe, as the modern world began to emerge, some Jews contributed strong banking and other financial skills.

All these skills were of use in Europe and were part of the whole body of skills that Jews brought with them to the New World.

There were great artistic talents, as well. In Spain, in Germany, in Russia—in all the lands from which Jews came to America—there were Jewish painters, sculptors, writers, and performers of all kinds. Their talents were part of the Jewish heritage, as successive waves of Jewish immigrants began to arrive in their new country. In all, Jews brought a tremendous heritage with them to America, coming as it did out of their thousands of years of experience and growth in all the countries of the Old World.

2

The Old Country

The very names recorded here are strange,
Of foreign accent, and of different climes;
Alvares and Rivera interchange
With Abraham and Jacob of old times . . .

from *The Jewish Cemetery at Newport*
by Henry Wadsworth Longfellow

For most American immigrants, there is a single "old country." For the Japanese, it is Japan; for the Irish, Ireland; for the Italians, Italy. But for a few ethnic groups, such as the Jews, there is no single "old country." Rather, there are many countries, all together or in groups thought of as "the old country."

For some Jewish-Americans, the old country is Spain or Portugal, more than 300 years ago, with stopovers since then in places like Brazil or Holland. For most of those in the second great wave of Jewish immigration, the old country is Germany, as much as 150 years ago. For the huge wave of Eastern European Jews, who started coming a century ago and came until the mid-1920s, the old country is Russia, Poland, Hungary, or any of the other countries of Eastern Europe. For more recent Jewish immigrants, the old country may be the Soviet Union, some of the Arab countries of North Africa and the Middle East, or Israel.

And those are only some of the places from which Jews came to the United States. For the last century and a half, Jews have been emigrating to the United States from every country in Europe and from all the rest of the world. Every European country has or had a substantial Jewish community, and from every Jewish community people went to America.

7

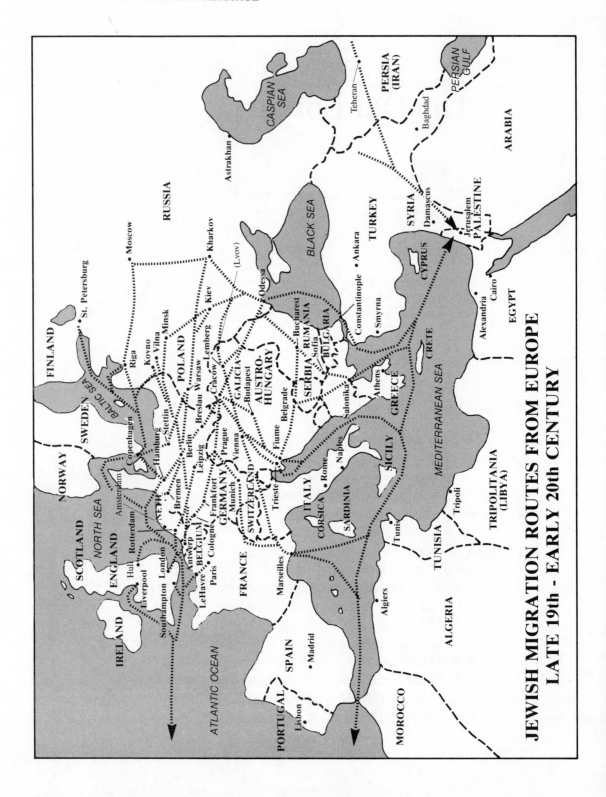

**JEWISH MIGRATION ROUTES FROM EUROPE
LATE 19th - EARLY 20th CENTURY**

Ireland, France, England, Scotland, Austria, Italy, and dozens of other countries have sent Jewish emigrants to America.

All the peoples of the world are met in America. So, too, are all the Jewish communities of the world. To understand how that happened, you have to know something about the history of the Jewish communities in "the old country."

Jews in the Ancient World

People of the Jewish faith were distributed throughout the ancient world. Many lived in Palestine and then in Egypt, from about 3,900 years ago. The Assyrians exiled a substantial Jewish community to the Iranian Plateau about 2,700 years ago. A very large Jewish community was in Babylonia from about 2,600 years ago. Jews traveled and traded the length and breadth of the ancient world, from China to the Atlantic and from the frozen north to the burning sands of the Sahara Desert.

In ancient times, as long as 500 years before the birth of Christ, a substantial Jewish community had begun to develop in Spain. Jews had come to Spain across the Mediterranean Sea with the Phoenicians, who had traded and settled there as early as 1000 B.C., over 3,000 years ago. By 600 B.C., the Phoenicians, now operating out of Carthage, in North Africa, had created a major city in Spain (now Cadiz), and a whole web of settlement and trading routes there.

By 200 B.C., Rome had defeated the Carthaginians and their great general, Hannibal, and had taken Spain. They did not greatly disturb the local populations, but rather ruled and took taxes from them. That local population of Spain included Jews.

The Jews were one of the many peoples conquered and ruled by Rome, in such colonies as Spain and also in the Jewish homeland of Judea. The Jews of the homeland revolted against Roman rule again and again—as did other Jewish communities all around the southern rim of the Mediterranean—without success. Rome was too strong.

The net result was a wide dispersal—called the *Diaspora*—of Jews, who arrived as refugees in many parts of the Roman world, and beyond. Spain was one of the few areas little touched by all this. There the Jewish community continued to develop and flourish, all during Roman times.

Jewish and Greek traders also went into other lands conquered by

In early 20th-century Palestine, this Jewish high priest and his sons displayed an ancient copy of the Pentateuch, the first five books of the Old Testament of the Bible.
(Library of Congress)

Rome, as did the traders of many other Roman-ruled nations. Small Jewish communities, for example, lived in southern France in the first through fifth centuries A.D. In Germany, Jewish traders lived and worked on the Rhine in the same period, and a Jewish community was to be found in Cologne in the fourth century A.D.

Roots of Persecution

By the early seventh century A.D., Catholicism had triumphed on the mainland of Western Europe. With it came a period of persecution for the Jews. During Roman times, many Jews had been rebels. They were often exiled and otherwise penalized for their rebellions. But they were seen by the Romans only as rebels. Later, in Moslem times, Jews were in some periods penalized for their faith by fundamentalist Moslems, as were other non-Moslems. But it was only in Christian Europe that Jews were persecuted as "Christ-killers," to be massacred and exiled again and again for many centuries.

The murder of some six million European Jews by the German Nazi government in the 20th century was the last and by far the worst of the European Jewish massacres. It was easy for the Nazis to make scapegoats out of the Jews of Europe because of all the prejudice that had gone before. Much of European Jewish history turns upon the fact of that prejudice.

To a large extent, Jews did what they did, lived as they lived, and went where they went because of that prejudice. That many Western European Jews became moneylenders, and few became farmers, was because they were in many places barred by law from farming—and also from the main professions and crafts. That Jews in many cities of the Middle Ages and beyond lived in the segregated, Jews-only sections, or ghettos—the infamous places back into which the Nazis later forced them—was due to that prejudice. That Jews in many European times and places could not be citizens, vote, hold office, or exercise any of the civil and political rights we now tend to take for granted was due to that prejudice. That Jewish communities were pushed all around Europe, here destroyed and there rebuilding again, was due to that prejudice. Similarly, that Jews came to America when they did, and in such numbers, had a great deal to do with the prejudices they encountered in the countries they came from.

Not all the times were dark, however. In France and Central Europe, that period of early persecution ended in 800 A.D., when Charles the

Great, or Charlemagne, became the Holy Roman Emperor. On the Iberian Peninsula, it ended in 711 A.D., when Moslem Arabs crossed from North Africa and took Spain and Portugal.

The Golden Age of the Spanish Jews

For Spain, the Moslem conquest began a Golden Age. In 755 A.D., Abd Ar Rahman, the first of the great Spanish Moslem Caliphs, ruled Spain from Córdoba. That city and all Moslem Spain became the greatest center of learning and culture in Europe. For centuries, Moslems, Jews, and Christians would live side by side in peace and mutual respect. Indeed, some houses of worship served all three religions at the same time, for each had a different holy day during the week.

For European Jews, the Moslem period in Spain was a golden age. Jews moved freely in Spanish society, as scholars, physicians, diplomats, writers, and advisers to caliphs and kings. These were the times of such eminent Jews as Hasdai Ibn Shaprut, physician and adviser to Abd Ar Rahman III, and the poets Judah Halevi and Solomon Ibn Gabirol. And of the great Jewish philosopher Moses Maimonides, who brought together all of the elements of the Talmud—the Jewish commentaries on the Old Testament—and at the same time infused Jewish thought with the humanism of the Greek philosopher Aristotle.

The Khazars

It was through the correspondence of Hasdai Ibn Shaprut that Western Europe learned of the Jewish Khazars. After the fall of Rome in the West, the Roman capital city became Constantinople (Byzantium). When the many Jews living there began to be persecuted by Christians, many fled north to the neighboring country of Khazaria.

The Khazars were a Turkic-speaking people of mixed background, one of the scores of peoples who have moved out of Asia into Europe throughout history. Much of the history of Eurasia is the movement of such peoples out of the Asian heartland and into the more highly developed lands around them. From the seventh through the tenth centuries A.D., the Khazars ruled a considerable empire north of the Caspian and Black seas, in what is now the southwestern Soviet Union. During the seventh and eighth centuries, the Khazars successfully fought a hundred-year war against the invading Arab armies, stopping the Arabs and turning them away from Eastern Europe, just as the Franks turned them away from Western Europe during the same period. The Khazar Empire became very powerful, standing in southwestern Asia astride one branch of the great Silk Road east to China—and exacting tribute from all who passed.

In about 740 A.D., the Khazar king, most of the nobility, and many others in the kingdom converted en masse to Judaism, creating the first independent Jewish state since ancient times. From our distance, and with at best sketchy sources, we do not really know why. Some have guessed that it was to counterbalance the pressure to convert to either Christianity or Mohammedanism, and so to preserve their independence. Whatever the motives for conversion, this Jewish state was powerful for several centuries, then lasted in weakened form until the Mongol conquest of the 12th century.

There is considerable dispute as to how much of the Jewish population of Russia and the rest of Eastern Europe came from this converted Khazar state, and how much came from Jews fleeing from Western Europe eastward during the Middle Ages. Whatever the proportions, it is clear that the Jews of Eastern Europe, like all the peoples of Eurasia, are a mixture of many peoples. In this, they are like Americans; the making of the marvelous mosaic that is the American people did not begin in North America.

Europe's Middle Ages

As to the Jews of Western Europe—flee they did. The period of peace during and after Charlemagne's reign was all too brief. By the middle of the 11th century, local anti-Jewish activity was widespread. And at the end of the 11th century, in 1096, came the First Crusade, ushering in several centuries of massacres and expulsions from most of the Catholic countries of Western and Central Europe.

During the First Crusade, the Crusaders slaughtered tens of thousands of Jews as they made their way east across Europe. Some of the worst massacres were in Metz, Worms, Mayence, the Rhine valley, and Prague.

Ultimately, in 1099, these Crusaders also massacred thousands of Jews in Jerusalem.

Massacres, expulsions, and other punitive actions were to continue for four centuries, only tapering off with the beginning of the modern era. In those centuries, Jews were routinely accused of such atrocities as ritual murder, aid to the Mongols, spreading the bubonic plague epidemic known as the Black Death, and much, much more. They were expelled from England in 1290; from the Holy Roman Empire, which included Germany, in 1298 and 1348; from France in 1306, 1322, and 1394; from Austria in 1421. And from Spain in 1492 and Portugal in 1497.

Yes, even from Spain, for the Christians had reconquered Spain from the Moslems. Christopher Columbus began his first voyage to the New World from the little Spanish port of Palos because the main port, Cadiz, was full of ships taking expelled Jews out of Spain.

Expulsion from Spain and Portugal

For centuries, Spain had seemed immune to the storm of anti-Jewish prejudice that swept the rest of Europe. Even during the long Spanish-Moslem wars for control of the many Spanish states, both sides had tended to accept Jews as valued members of their communities.

But early in the 14th century, anti-Jewish feelings were growing in the Christian states of Spain, with discriminatory laws and massacres following. By 1375, there were anti-Jewish laws in all the Christian states, and in 1391 a full-scale countrywide massacre, in which tens of thousands of Jews were killed. Hundreds of thousands of other Jews converted to Christianity to escape this Spanish holocaust. From then on, these converts were called *Conversos* (converteds), or "New Christians." They were also insultingly called *Marranos*, a Spanish term for swine.

Many Conversos, although often secret believers in Judaism, rose to positions of power and influence in Spanish life during the next century. However, anti-Jewish and anti-Converso feeling continued strong throughout Christian Spain. There were new massacres of Jews in 1474 and 1475. In 1478, the Vatican appointed the first Inquisitors, and by 1480 the Catholic Church in Spain was burning Conversos at the stake for their supposed heresies. This murder of those who were judged to be false

Catholics, and many other dissenters, too, was the infamous Inquisition. The remaining 150,000 Jews of Spain were expelled in 1492, while the Inquisition continued against Conversos and others accused of being heretics.

About 100,000 Spanish Jews went to Portugal, only to be expelled from that country five years later. By 1500, the Jews of Spain and Portugal had been scattered the length and breadth of the Mediterranean, from the Italian states to Salonika, in Greece, to Turkey, to North Africa. Some later went north, to the Protestant Low Countries, which gave refuge to small groups of Spanish Jews.

These Spanish Jews were also known as *Sephardic* Jews, who followed the Spanish-Jewish religious rites. All other Jews were known as *Ashkenazi* Jews, who followed the German-Jewish religious rites. A few Sephardic Jews went to Brazil, either as Jews or as Conversos who later reconverted to Judaism. We will meet these Brazilian-Spanish Jews later on, for a few of them were among the first Jews to settle in North America.

It is these Spanish Jews who formed the new Jewish communities in Western Europe at the beginning of the great age of European exploration of the New World. By the end of the 16th century there was a small, but thriving Spanish Jewish community in Amsterdam. In 1622, Jews were welcomed by King Christian IV of Denmark. Several of the Italian city-states also welcomed Jews in this period. And in 1657, Oliver Cromwell welcomed Jews back into England, almost four centuries after their expulsion. The Spanish Jews made up the first wave of Jewish immigrants to North America.

Jews in Eastern Europe

In Eastern Europe, a refuge had opened up much earlier. From the 12th through the 16th centuries, a very large, vigorous set of Jewish communities developed in Poland. By the middle of the 17th century, there were an estimated 500,000 Jews in Poland. They engaged in a wide variety of occupations and enjoyed a considerable measure of independence, as compared with the Jews of Germany and France. But there was much anti-Semitism, as well, with ghettos in some cities and an increasing number of economic and political restrictions.

That anti-Semitism bore bitter fruit during the Cossack uprising of

1648. The Cossacks, a Slavic people living in southern Russia, rose under Bogdan Chmielnicki against the Poles in the Ukraine, and in the course of the uprising killed tens of thousands of Jews. Then, in 1654, the Russians attacked Poland from the east, and in 1655 the Swedes attacked Poland from the West. During the local uprisings that followed, many more Jews were killed. In the next century, local attacks continued and grew, culminating in the massacre of tens of thousands more Jews in 1768.

The result of it all was the creation of a new body of Jewish refugees. These refugees moved westward into Germany, Austria, and the rest of Central Europe, as the modern period began and the condition of Jews eased in those countries. From this Jewish population came the second wave of Jewish emigrants to America.

In spite of their adverse situation, large numbers of Jews remained in Eastern Europe and Russia, some perhaps being descendants of the Khazars. It is from these large Jewish populations that the third, and main, wave of Jews came to America.

A New Day in Western Europe

By the beginning of the 18th century, a new wind was beginning to blow through Europe. England still had a king, but his powers were diminishing and democracy was on the rise. The French king still ruled absolutely, but there were philosophers who wrote of democracy, and there was a democratic revolution being born. People in many independent states of Germany and Italy were beginning to talk of freedom. Everywhere in Western and Central Europe, kings, nobles, and old religious leaders were facing great changes.

The new ideas of freedom and equality under the law—the same ideas that were to inspire the American Revolution in 1776 and the French Revolution in 1789—brought a wholly new kind of freedom to the Jews of the United States and of Western and Central Europe. In the Low Countries, the Sephardic Jewish community had grown all during the 17th and 18th centuries. In England, a smaller Jewish community grew, one very important to America, for many European Jews came through London on their way to the British North American colonies. In France, large Jewish communities thrived, especially in the Alsace region, and were ready to join the revolution when it came. In Germany, Jews led by

Moses Mendelssohn began to modernize Jewish life and literature, and to work with many of the leaders of the German states to ease the poor treatment of Jews in Germany.

German Jew Moses Mendelssohn (grandfather of composer Felix Mendelssohn) was a leader of the Reform movement in Europe in the 18th century. (Library of Congress)

But it was the French Revolution of 1789 that really provided a new dawn for the Jews of Western and Central Europe. With the revolution and its Declaration of the Rights of Man, the principle of equality for all was established. The genie of freedom was out of the bottle and could not be put back, however strong the reaction that later set in. In 1791, the Jews of France were granted full citizenship. In 1796, with French pressure, so were the Jews of Holland. In 1797, liberating French forces removed and burned the gates of the Jewish ghetto in Venice. In Rome, the old regime was overturned in 1798. In Germany, legal equality came as French armies took many of the German states.

Ultimately Napoleon and the French were defeated. After 1815, a reaction set in, especially in some German and Italian states. But it did not last long, for freedom was still in the air, for Jews among others. The French Revolution of 1830 assured the equality of French Jews. After the widespread revolutions of 1848 and through to the end of the century, Germany, Italy, and Austria-Hungary followed suit. In Britain, anti-Jewish restrictions were lifted by mid-century.

Not that it was all easy. The bitter prejudices of a thousand years are not wafted away with the stroke of a pen. There still remained an enormous reservoir of anti-Jewish prejudice throughout Europe. But the legal and moral basis for equality was laid by the French Revolution and what followed. The 19th century was therefore a period of liberation for the Jews of Western and Central Europe.

Repression in Eastern Europe

Not so to the east. At the beginning of the 19th century, in Russia and Russian-occupied Poland, there were about one and a half million Jews. This was by far the largest Jewish population in the world. And it was held by the most repressive government in Europe—repressive to all its peoples, by the way, not just to Jews. But it was the Jews who were singled out for the worst treatment.

Actually it was, in a certain sense, an accident of history that Russia had such a large Jewish population. Although large numbers of Jews lived in Russia's outer provinces, Jews had been expelled from central Russia in 1727, 1739, and 1742. Then, between 1772 and 1795, Poland was attacked and split up among Russia, Prussia, and Austria. Russia's very

The Jews have always been "the people of the book." Even poor towns in the Pale had a heder, *or Hebrew school for boys, like this one in Polotsk, in Russian Poland.* (From The Promised Land by Mary Antin, 1912)

large share of what had been Poland contained about one million Jews, the largest single Jewish population in the world.

In 1791, Catherine the Great created the Pale of Settlement, which included much of the Ukraine and the Russian-occupied part of Poland. Most of the Jews of Russia and Poland were forced into this area. During the Napoleonic Wars at the beginning of the 19th century, there was an easing of restrictions upon Russian and Polish Jews. But after 1815, as reaction swept Europe, the Russian government introduced many new anti-Jewish laws and restrictions.

What developed in the Pale of Settlement was the large, persecuted Russian Jewish community from which came the third and by far the largest wave of Jewish emigration into the United States. It was a Yiddish-speaking community, Yiddish being the Jewish dialect developed in the Middle Ages, a mixture of medieval German dialects and bits and pieces of several other languages. And this was the community of the *shtetls*, the many small villages in the Pale, into which hundreds of thousands of Jews were forced. These were the kinds of communities brought to life so appealingly in the musical *Fiddler on the Roof*.

But the facts of life in the Pale were not so appealing. The vast majority of the Jews in the Pale were desperately poor, and were barred from owning and working the land. The economy was stagnant, the ways of making a living were very limited, and modern education was almost impossible to secure. The Russian Czar ruled, and there were no real political and civil rights. For Jews, this was a place of constant uncertainty and oppression, where anti-Jewish violence was common, young children were routinely impressed into the Czar's army, money was always scarce—and it might be much worse tomorrow.

Life in the Pale was mainly a country life, although some Jews worked in such Polish cities as Warsaw. But there were many Russian Jews outside the Pale, as well, mainly in the cities of southern Russia, such as Kiev and Novgorod. As Russia began to industrialize in the 19th century, more Jews went into the Russian cities, as factory workers, skilled craftworkers, teachers, merchants, and innkeepers. What happened, though, was that as new Russian restrictive laws went into effect late in the 19th century, many of these Jews outside the Pale were forced into it, crowding this main area of Jewish settlement even further, and making it even harder to make a living there. But first there was a thaw.

In 1855, Alexander II became Czar of Russia. Responding to the new wave of liberal thought sweeping Europe, he introduced many reforms. He made a serious attempt to bring Russia into the modern world, among other major acts liberating tens of millions of serfs and easing many anti-Jewish restrictions. Most Jews were still forced to live in the Pale of Settlement, but the main Russian cities were opened to some kinds of Jewish professionals and merchants, and the universities were opened to Jews.

But Alexander II was assassinated on March 13, 1881, and the period of reform abruptly ended. In April and May of that year, there were anti-Jewish riots called *pogroms* throughout southeastern Russia. In May 1882, the Russian government instituted the May Laws, far more severely restricting Russian and Polish Jews than ever before in modern times.

Restrictions and pogroms continued. During one pogrom in Kishinev in 1903, hundreds of Jews died. Tens of thousands of Russian Jews died in pogroms between then and the outbreak of the First World War in 1914.

These later pogroms were carried out mainly by the "Black Hundreds," semiofficial bands organized by the Russian government to make scapegoats of the Jews. For by now, the Russian government badly needed scapegoats. From the 1890s on, there was revolution in the Russian air. Dozens of liberal and radical groups were formed all during the period, and an unsuccessful revolution was attempted in 1905. Jews participated in both socialist and Zionist movements, as well as in groups aiming to overthrow the Czar.

These eight children, who arrived in America from Russia in 1908, had been orphaned in the pogroms, the widespread massacres of the Jews. (American Museum of Immigration, Statue of Liberty National Monument, National Park Service, U.S. Department of the Interior, Sherman Collection)

After the sharp anti-Jewish turn of 1881 and 1882, a good many Jews became Zionists, who believed that Palestine had been and should again be a national Jewish homeland, and went there to build what eventually became the state of Israel. Millions of other Jews stayed in Russia and ultimately helped bring down the government. And millions more—some two and a half million in all—went to America.

3

We Hold These Truths

We hold these truths to be self-evident, that all men are created equal, that they are endowed by their Creator with certain inalienable Rights, that among these are Life, Liberty, and the pursuit of Happiness . . .

These words from *The Declaration of Independence*, July 4, 1776, have been called a beacon, a flame, a magnet drawing people to America from all over the world. And so they are. *The idea of freedom as a matter of right* was extraordinary when it was put forward in 1776. It is extraordinary even today, when most of humankind still has far too little political, religious, and economic freedom.

In America, this idea of freedom was abroad long before 1776. It came with the Pilgrims, in 1620. At Provincetown, on Cape Cod, all the able-bodied male immigrants on the *Mayflower* signed the Mayflower Compact, providing for political equality among them. Yes, the women were left out, and that is a sad omission by our modern standards. But it did establish the principle of equality for the first time on American soil, and in a way most unusual in the world at that time. And it also marked the beginning of a new kind of society, in which the government pledged itself not only to uphold the rights of the citizens, but also to *serve* those citizens, not rule over them.

For Jews, North America was from the start a place where there was a chance to be free. How different that was from the Old World! Why did Jews come to America? First of all, last of all, from the earliest times until today, to be free. To know something about Jewish history is to know that Jews have for thousands of years fought, bled, and moved as necessary

Jewish-American Emma Lazarus celebrated the meaning of freedom to European immigrants in her poem, "The New Colossus," carved into the pedestal of the Statue of Liberty.
(Library of Congress)

again and again to find even a relatively small amount of freedom. For Jews, then, America has been from the first a haven, a place of refuge where political equality, freedom of worship, and economic opportunity were all possible. And all at the same time. Surely, not without encountering anti-Semitism and having to struggle for equality. But always with a very good chance of success, which was very different from the Jewish experience in Europe.

The way the first group of Jews came to North America is symbolic of all who followed. For they came in flight, on the run from the Spanish and Portuguese, seeking new homes, and with no way back.

By 1630, almost a century and a half after the expulsion of the Jews from Spain and Portugal, there was a substantial Jewish community in Holland. By then, the Portuguese held Brazil and Spain held most of the rest of South and Central America. In that year, 1630, a Dutch expeditionary force took the Brazilian coastal province of Pernambuco, and with it the port of Recife. There were Dutch-Jewish soldiers and merchants with the expeditionary force and Spanish and Portuguese Conversos (New Christians) in the conquered areas of Brazil. As more Dutch Jews came to Recife and many Conversos reconverted to Judaism, a strong community of about 1,000 Jews developed in the city of Recife.

But it did not last very long. In 1654, the Portuguese drove the Dutch out of Brazil. Rather than again face the Catholic Inquisition, the Jewish community of Recife fled. Some went to Holland, and others to the Dutch territories in and around the Caribbean. And a few found their way to the Dutch West India Company's colony of New Amsterdam (later New York). In September 1654, the French frigate *Saint Catherine* entered New Amsterdam harbor, carrying 23 penniless Jewish refugees from Brazil. Actually, they were somewhat less than penniless. On arrival, all their possessions were sold to pay part of what they owed the French for their passage—and they were still in debt.

Only two other Jews were in New Amsterdam at the time, Jacob Barsimonson and Salomon Pietersen. Both had arrived on August 22, less than a month before. These two and the 23 from Brazil were to found the first Jewish community in North America.

First, there was a battle to be won, for Peter Stuyvesant, governor of New Amsterdam, wanted to expel the 23 Brazilian Jews. Stuyvesant wrote to the Company, making some very familiar charges. He described the Jews as engaged in "their customary usury," and at the same time described himself as "fearing that owing to their present indigence they might become a charge in the coming winter." He told the Company that he had "deemed it useful to require them in a friendly way to depart." And he "prayed . . . that the deceitful race—such hateful enemies and blasphemers of the name of Christ—be not allowed further to infect and trouble this new colony . . ."

It was the Jews of Amsterdam who responded. They strongly pointed out to the directors of the Dutch West India Company that these Brazilian Jews could not "go to Spain or Portugal because of the Inquisition." Further, that the "Jewish nation in Brazil have at all times been faithful and have striven to guard and maintain that place, risking for that purpose their possessions and their blood." And last, "that many of the Jewish nation are principal shareholders in the Company."

In the circumstances, humanity, loyalty—and shareholding—won the day. The directors wrote to Stuyvesant, reversing his expulsion of the Jews, because of "the considerable loss sustained by this nation [meaning the Jews], with others, in the taking of Brazil, as also because of the large amount of capital which they still have invested in the shares of this company." There would be other battles for equality as the Jewish community in New Amsterdam began to grow. But the first American Jewish community had been started.

The British Colonies

Such battles did not need to be fought in Rhode Island. For there, in 1636, Roger Williams had founded a community that was extraordinary at the time for its religious freedom. In 1657, Oliver Cromwell had welcomed the Jews back into England after almost four centuries of exclusion—though with considerable restrictions. In 1658, Jews from Holland began to settle in Rhode Island, and especially in Newport. From the first, they were freer in New England than anywhere in Europe. Later, many more Jews came, from Holland, from the British and Dutch territories in and around the Caribbean, and from England. Those coming from the south and from Holland were mainly Sephardic, that is, Spanish and Portuguese Jews. Some of those who came from England were also Spanish and Portuguese in origin. Others coming through England from northern Europe were Ashkenazi. From such countries as Germany and Poland they, too, began to seek political, religious, and economic freedom in America.

For no matter how free a Jew was in the Old World, there were always restrictions. Restrictions on voting, on holding office, on attempting to convert others to their faith, on the kind of occupations they could enter, on where they could live, on whom they could marry. There were restrictions in the British North American colonies, too, but they were far less disabling, and clearly on their way out, as the spirit of democracy developed in the Colonies.

And so it was that the largest Jewish community in the Colonies grew and flourished in Newport. New Jewish immigrants from Europe developed smaller, quite stable communities in Savannah, Philadelphia, and Charleston, as well. And in New York, after the Dutch were supplanted by the English in 1664, a small Jewish community continued to grow all during Colonial times. By 1776, there were 2,000 to 3,000 Jews in the new United States.

The Golden Land

With the Revolution, America became for Jews by far the freest place in the world. Yet, although individuals and sometimes families continued to immigrate to America, no mass movement to America occurred. That was because of the French Revolution and the Napoleonic Wars that followed. Between 1789 and 1815, Europeans were engaged in what for them was a world war. Young men were in the massive armies of the warring countries. Travel to America was also severely restricted by wartime conditions. After 1815, there was a reaction to the new freedoms brought by the French Revolution. But even so, the condition of Jews in Western and Central Europe was considerably improved. In Germany, for example, where the largest Central European Jewish populations were located, many economic opportunities opened up in those years.

Yet there were still restrictions, and a growing feeling throughout Europe that America was, indeed, a golden land. With progress toward freedom comes great impatience to be even more free. America offered freedoms such as Jews in Germany and the rest of Central Europe could not see coming for many decades.

Material things changed, too. As Germany and the rest of Central Europe began to industrialize, large numbers of people left the land, mov-

This Jewish emigrant, a vegetarian, left Russia rather than serve in the czar's army and be forced to give up his religious convictions and his special diet. (American Museum of Immigration, Statue of Liberty National Monument, National Park Services, U.S. Department of the Interior, Sherman Collection)

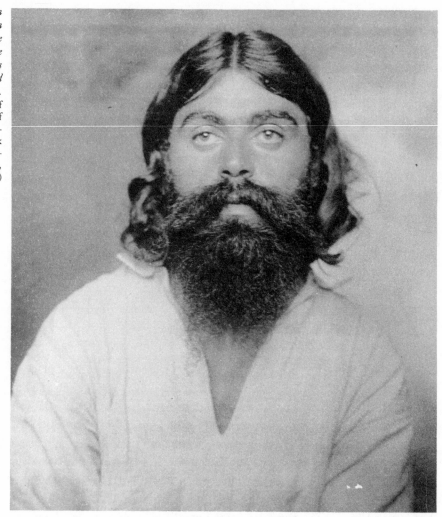

ing to the new jobs available in the cities. Suddenly, people were far less well-rooted than they had been, and far readier to move, whether to Berlin or Baltimore.

It also began to be much easier and less expensive to go to America. Steam-powered ships began to cross the Atlantic regularly in the 1820s, and by the 1840s were becoming much bigger, faster, and less expensive than sailing ships. Steamboats began appearing on European and American rivers in the 1820s and 1830s, making travel on both continents cheaper and quicker. And by the 1850s, a network of railroads had begun to cover both Europe and North America.

On top of all that, the immigrant "chains" began to grow. It has worked the same way for all the ethnic groups that have come to America in the last three and a half centuries. First, one member of a family comes. Or a single family from a village. Some money is made, enough to send passage expenses, and perhaps a little more, to those left behind, along with glowing letters about how wonderful it is in America. These "immigration letters" or "America letters" are known to every ethnic group. Soon there are many people talking about coming to America, guidebooks telling about America and how to get there, agents recruiting for shipping companies, and employers recruiting for American jobs—and the rush is on.

In some ethnic groups, the result has properly been called "American fever." Then, whole families go to America, and whole villages, and most of the people in whole districts of the country. It happened in Ireland, Italy, Scandinavia, Poland—and, for extremely powerful reasons, to the Jews of Central, and then of Eastern Europe, starting early in the 19th century. Mainly from Germany and Austria-Hungary, an estimated 200,000 to 300,000 Jews immigrated to America between 1830 and 1880, with tens of thousands more beginning to stream out of Eastern Europe in the 1880s.

While heavy German and Central European immigration to the United States continued all through the 19th century, Jewish immigration slowed after the 1870s. In this period, democracy was on the rise in Germany, and with it conditions improved greatly for Jews. The vast majority of German Jews from then until the rise of Hitler in the 1930s decided to work out their lives at home, in Germany. Had they poured out of Germany to America then, as they had earlier in the 19th century, many more would have survived. But that part of the story comes later.

Refugees

As early as the 1860s, some Jews were coming to America out of Poland, then partitioned among Russia, Germany, and Austria-Hungary. But it was in the 1880s, after the assassination of Czar Alexander II and the restrictive May Laws of 1882, that Jews began to leave Russia in great numbers. During the 1880s and 1890s, many tens of thousands of Jews left Russia and other Eastern European countries every year. By the early years of the 20th century, there were usually over 100,000 Jews leaving those countries annually. Some went to France, Great Britain, and other European countries. Tens of thousands went much farther, to Canada, Australia, South Africa, and South America. Most, though, came to the United States, in a flood tide of immigrants over 10 times as large as all the Jewish-American immigration until then.

From humiliation and harassment—as here Nazi soldiers forcibly shave a Jew's beard— the German war machine turned to murder on a previously unknown scale. (Library of Congress, Inter-allied Information Center)

*Refugees came to
America from all parts
of the world; this
Armenian Jew escaped
Turkish persecution in
the mid-1920s.*
(Photo by Lewis W.
Hine, New York Public
Library)

   These Jews were both refugees from oppression and seekers of a new life full of the opportunities that were denied them in what had been their home countries. A few of them went back to Russia to help make a revolution against the Czar in 1917, but only a few. The vast majority came and stayed, finding the freedom and opportunity they sought.

   When you have no peace, nor bread, nor land, nor hope for the future—and all those things seem possible in America—you go. And then you send back for your family, your friends, and their families and friends. That is what the Jews of Eastern Europe did. Millions came; millions more would have come, if not for World War I and the American immigration restrictions that followed, which effectively shut the Golden Door to emigrants from eastern and southern Europe, including those millions of Jews. No matter how difficult the trip, they came and kept coming as long as they could. No, the streets were not paved with gold—and they knew that. But in America you could be free—free to be an equal citizen, to vote, to worship or not as you please, to follow any occupation at all for as far as it might take you. And all without the Czar, the nobility, the police, the Black Hundreds, the pogroms, and the constant fear of what tomorrow might bring.

4

Voyage to the Golden Door

Not like the brazen giant of Greek fame,
With conquering limbs astride from land to land;
Here at our sea-washed, sunset gates shall stand
A mighty woman with a torch, whose flame
Is the imprisoned lightning, and her name
Mother of Exiles. From her beacon-hand
Glows world-wide welcome; her mild eyes command
The air-bridged harbor that twin cities frame.
"Keep ancient lands, your storied pomp!" cries she
With silent lips. "Give me your tired, your poor,
Your huddled masses yearning to breathe free,
The wretched refuse of your teeming shore.
Send these, the homeless, tempest-tost to me,
I lift my lamp beside the golden door!"

The New Colossus,
by Emma Lazarus

The coming to America was part of the greatest migration in human history. It was not a large migration for the first two centuries after the English landed at Jamestown and Plymouth, perhaps 1,000,000 to 2,000,000 people in all. But between the 1830s and the closing of the golden door through American immigration restriction in the 1920s, fully 35,000,000 people came to the United States. About 2,500,000 to 3,000,000 of them were Jews, and most of those Jews came out of Eastern Europe between the 1880s and the 1920s.

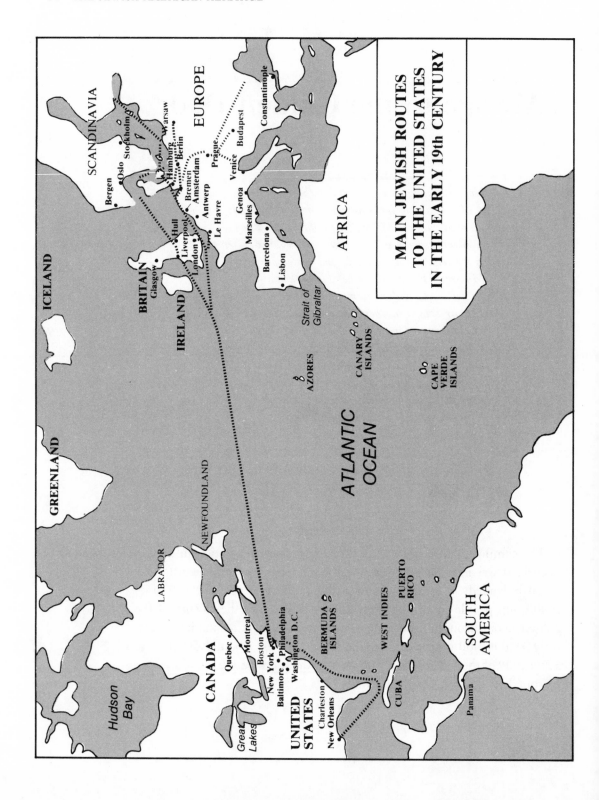

MAIN JEWISH ROUTES
TO THE UNITED STATES
IN THE EARLY 19th CENTURY

Sailing to America

During the first two centuries, a considerable portion of those few Jews who did immigrate to America came from the south, as had the refugees of 1654. These were mainly Spanish and Portuguese Jews and Conversos. Some Conversos continued to emigrate from Brazil, to convert back to Judaism once they escaped the shadow of the Inquisition. Some sailed north from the Dutch colonies in Dutch Guiana and Curaçao. These were generally either refugees from Brazil or Jews who had traveled directly from Holland. Some came north from the British colonies in Jamaica, Barbados, and English Guiana.

For those coming from the south in this way, the voyage was a relatively easy one, even in the tiny sailing ships of those times. The wind and the currents were often favorable, and much of the journey proceeded north along the coast of North America.

For those emigrating from Europe, across the stormy North Atlantic, the voyage was far rougher and longer. And European Jews coming to America in those centuries often faced a long land journey, as well. A few sailed directly from England, but most Jews bound for the British North American colonies traveled much farther. Before the coming of the steamboat and the railroad, it might take a month to make your way out of Poland or southern Germany to one of the North German ports, on foot and with your possessions in a cart. Then there might be weeks of waiting for a small sailing ship to take you to England. Then another long wait in Liverpool for one of the tiny transatlantic sailing ships. Until the 1820s, most of such transatlantic voyages were unscheduled. Instead, ships' captains waited until they had enough paying cargo, including immigrants, and then set sail.

After all that, poor immigrants could expect to spend perhaps two months in "steerage"—that is, in the upper hold of that tiny, pitching sailing ship. There would be little food, and what there was would be poor and often badly spoiled. There would be little water, as well, and thirst was often a huge problem. There would almost inevitably be seasickness, for these were very often inland people, quite unused to the sea. Also, there would often be lice, and all the minor illnesses that afflict weakened people who are eating and drinking badly. And all too often there would also be an outbreak of major epidemic diseases on the ships, such as the dreaded typhus and cholera. In all, immigration to America has always been a huge

In boats like these, the first Jewish refugees from Brazil made their way to New Amsterdam (now New York) in 1654.
(Library of Congress)

undertaking, involving a break with a whole way of life. But in the days of sail, it was also an extremely dangerous undertaking, and many did not survive the crossing.

Part of the problem was the North Atlantic itself. The main currents and winds simply run the wrong way for sailing ships coming from Europe to North America. That is why Columbus sailed to Central America. He was following the main currents and winds south, and then across the Atlantic. Later explorers and traders did the same, following currents and winds up the coast of the Americas and then back to Europe across the North Atlantic. Coming the other way, as from Liverpool to New York, it took sailing ships twice as long to sail from Europe to America as it did to sail back again.

The Pace Quickens

In the 1830s, the pace of emigration from Europe to the United States quickened, and with it the demand for larger, regularly scheduled ships across the North Atlantic. From 1830 through 1870, 2,267,000 Germans are recorded as coming to the United States. Among them were an estimated 200,000 to 300,000 German Jews. Immigration statistics are kept by nationality, so that the number of Jews entering the United States must, in all periods, be an estimate. Because of the long and complicated history of the Jews, it is quite right to see them as often members of more than one ethnic group—for example, as German and Jewish, or Spanish and Jewish, or Jewish and Polish.

As Jewish immigration grew, it became far more organized. From the 1820s on, many Jews came out of Germany in groups. Individuals might travel across Germany to such north German cities as Mainz, and from there go on to the main Northern European ports. Most went directly to such ports as Bremen and Hamburg in Germany; Rotterdam and Amsterdam, in Holland; and Le Havre in France. From those ports, most sailed directly to the United States, though smaller numbers went to France, England, Canada, Australia, and many other countries. Some of those who went to England did not stay, but rather made their way to Liverpool, there to board immigrant ships bound for North America. During this period, Liverpool was still the largest port for emigration from Europe. It was the main departure port for British and Irish emigrants, and also a major port for Scandinavians and Germans.

Now immigration to America was no longer a matter of occasional small packet boats waiting for cargo and immigrants. From 1818 on, many of the strong, square-rigged sailing ships used in the North Atlantic were called "liners," rather than "packets." They had become parts of shipping "lines"—that is, groups of many ships, with scheduled departures and arrivals, as shipping lines and airlines have to this day. And the ships became larger and faster. By the middle of the 19th century, the average Europe-to-America trip across the North Atlantic was no longer two months, but an average of only 36 days.

In the 1840s, and especially after the unsuccessful democratic European revolutions of 1848, Jews came out of Europe to America in ever-increasing numbers. Now German Jews were being joined by substantial bodies of German-speaking Jews from throughout the Austro-Hungarian empire. Their feelings were best expressed by Jewish-Bohemian writer Leopold Kompert, who wrote a widely circulated article called "On To America!": "No help has come to us! The sun of freedom has risen for the Fatherland; for us it is merely a bloody northern light . . . Let us go to America!"

The Steamship Era

In the 1840s, many of the immigrants were coming across the North Atlantic in steamships, rather than sailing ships. By the late 1850s, the steamships in use were in the 3,000- to 4,000-ton range, several times as large as the sailing packets being used in the North Atlantic. These relatively large steamships were by then routinely crossing the North Atlantic from Europe to North America in 10 to 12 days, one-third the time the sailing ships had taken. These steamships were to be the main immigrant carriers until the airlines took over in the 1950s.

As the Jewish emigration from the German-speaking countries grew, organizations were formed to assist the emigrants. In the late 1840s, emigration societies were set up in Vienna, Prague, Budapest, and Lemberg (Lvov). Such organizations were the forerunners of the large international associations that were later to help millions of Jews cross Europe and the North Atlantic on their way out of Russia and Eastern Europe.

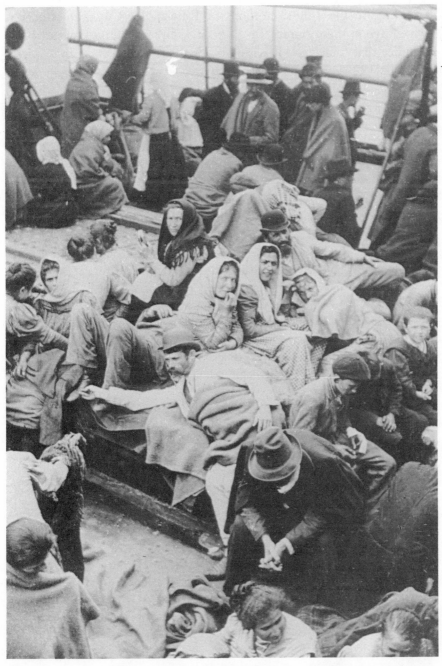

When weather permitted, steerage passengers would come up on deck for a bit of fresh air, wrapped in their coats and shawls. (National Park Service, U.S. Department of the Interior)

Russian Exodus

Starting in the 1880s, millions of Russian Jews went to America. Driven from their homes by pogroms, by restrictive laws, by the prejudice that fouled the Russian air, they left Russia for a freer place. From the 1880s on, the Russian restrictions against Jews became worse and worse—and the "American fever" grew and grew, as those who had gone to America wrote home, sent tickets and money, and urged those left behind to come and join them. Writer Mary Antin, who emigrated from Russia to the United States in 1891, tells of how it was at home in Russia:

It was a little before Passover that the cry of the hunted thrilled the Jewish world with the familiar fear. The wholesale expulsion of Jews from Moscow and its surrounding district at cruelly short notice was the name of this latest disaster. Where would the doom strike next? The Jews who lived illegally without [outside] the Pale turned their possessions into cash and slept in their clothes, ready for immediate flight. Those who lived in the comparative security of the Pale trembled for their brothers and sisters without, and opened wide their doors to afford the fugitives refuge. And hundreds of fugitives, preceded by a wail of distress, flocked into the open district, bringing their trouble where trouble was never absent, mingling their tears with the tears that never dried.

The open cities becoming thus suddenly crowded, every man's chance of making a living was diminished in proportion to the number of additional competitors. Hardship, acute distress, ruin for many: thus spread the disaster, ring beyond ring, from the stone thrown by a despotic official into the ever-full river of Jewish persecution.

Passover was celebrated in tears that year. In the story of the Exodus we would have read a chapter of current history, only for us there was no deliverer and no promised land.

But what said some of us at the end of the long service? Not "May we be next year in Jerusalem," but "Next year—in America!" So there was our promised land, and many faces were turned towards the West. And if the waters of the Atlantic did not part for them, the wanderers rode its bitter flood by a miracle as great as any the rod of Moses ever wrought.

When the Czar's government made it difficult for Jews to leave, as by denying them passports, Jews left anyway. Some left legally, but a great many others left Russia by night, going across closed borders with only the clothes on their backs and what little they could carry—but often with that precious ticket to America in hand. In those years a whole network of emigrant guides helped Jews come across the borders and out of Russia. Some of the guides made a business of it, and some of them victimized many of the emigrants they took across the frontiers, taking their money and possessions, as well. But many guides safely and surely took their share of the millions of Jewish emigrants out of Russia.

It was often a very difficult journey, across miles of field, forest, and river, with the border guards always a great danger. Frequently they were bribed by the crossing guides, but no one could be sure that the crossing would go safely, even when the guards had been bribed not to shoot. The Russian winter made it still harder, even though some new crossings opened then, when the rivers were frozen and people could walk on the ice.

Nor was the journey out of Russia always a very carefully planned matter. Sometimes, events made it necessary to simply get out, as fast and as completely as possible. Here, for example, is the story of how Fanny Kligerman's family left Russia for America, one jump ahead of the Cossacks, as she remembered it three quarters of a century later:

> In Europe, I can remember the house where I was born, in a small town close to Kiev. We lived there quite comfortably—we weren't poor but we weren't rich. Food we always had on the table. And clothes. I didn't have six dresses, like now. In school, we had to wear uniforms, we couldn't wear anything else. So I had two—one to wear and one to wash. It was a small town, and everybody was comfortable, see?
>
> But every night the pogroms were all around. I hate to tell you. They were chasing us out. They were chasing after us, to kill everyone. I remember the pogroms, the Kishinev pogroms, how they frightened us to death. One night we were hidden in a basement with a two- or three-month-old baby. And we had to "shush, shh, shh" the baby. We said, "Keep still! Maybe somebody is going to hear us!" This I remember very well. We had working for us a girl, a Gentile girl—she had brought up my father yet. While we were hidden in the basement, she gave us food through a little crack. I'll never forget it.

The best friend my father had in his life came to see us one day. My father didn't recognize him and said, "Who are you?"

The man answered, "Don't you recognize me?"

My father said, "No."

The man said, "I'm so-and-so."

My father almost fell on the floor. His friend's hair had turned white—and he was only thirty-two years old. They had taken one of his children and tore her apart. They tied the child to a truck and another truck and they tore her apart.

One day there was a rumor that they are coming to us, the pogrommers. What are we going to do? My father took all the knives and the scissors and everything, and he buried them someplace, so they can't kill us. He had a friend, a lawyer, who said, "Look, we have nothing to lose. Let's do something." So we set tables outside—it was summer—we put tables out with plenty of whiskey. We would get them drunk and they would not touch us. And so it was. They came to the house with sacks to load, but they never made it. They all got drunk and they didn't bother us and they disappeared. He was clever, that lawyer.

But my father said, "That's going to be the end of it. We're going to get out. Let's get out while we're still alive." He sold the house as soon as I am talking to you—it didn't take two hours. The house was only a couple of months built. We had just got into it, but my father said, "I don't want to own anything. I want my family alive."

We left the same night. We went to somebody's home for supper, and we had to walk to the station about four miles to get a train. We were afraid, but nobody followed us. They were still drunk. You see, they got drunk when it was light yet, but we went through the night. We had to walk miles to run away from Europe, carrying our belongings—and diapers. My mother had such small children and I carried my youngest sister. She couldn't hold three children, so we had to help. We had a lot of little children among the seven families that traveled together, so we changed off. I was thirteen years old, and I had to carry a baby, and that is how we got out—all seven families.

We hated to leave. I had a grandfather and grandmother living in Europe and my father was an only child. It was terrible to part with the two of them, but they wouldn't go along. They wanted to die in Europe. My father said, "Why don't you want to live in another country?" No. So they died there. But we wanted them along.

Whatever the hazards, they came and kept coming. Despite Emma Lazarus's poem, at the beginning of this chapter, these were by no means the "wretched refuse" or "huddled masses" of Europe. For them, there was not the "dumb defeated resignation" some thought they saw when they arrived at the European ports exhausted by their trips across Europe. Far from it. These were some of the best people of their time, bright, strong, alert, and ready to walk across closely guarded borders by night and then across the whole face of Europe, if need be, to get to a ship that would take them to America. These were people who would build new lives and communities in America, in Great Britain, in Palestine, and all over the world. Later, their children and grandchildren would come back to Europe, part of the armies that would destroy the German Nazis.

Once out of such repressive countries as Russia and Rumania, Jews joined the huge stream of immigrants on their way to America. For Jews were far from the only ones coming to America in those days. Two and a half million Jews left Europe for America between the 1880s and the 1920s, but they were only a small part of the 20,000,000 Europeans who came to America in those years.

With that many people involved, immigration became a whole industry. That was so every step of the way, from villages deep in southern Russia all the way to the farthest reaches of North America. There were professional guides, railroads, innkeepers, food providers, shipping companies, government employees, welfare organization people—there were even the thieves who made a living by cheating and robbing immigrants.

In Europe, the Jewish immigrants would normally travel in groups, often taken all the way to the main European ports by guides or shipping company scouts. Most traveled by railroad, though for some years many Rumanian Jews traveled in groups that walked all the way across Europe—until their government was shamed into letting them leave with some of their money. On the long and difficult way across Europe, some Jews were helped by Jewish welfare organizations, which sometimes provided food and a place to stay. Most importantly, though, these organizations did their best to assure safe passage across Europe, by securing fair treatment from the Western European countries the Jews passed through. Some local Western European Jewish communities resisted the flood of Russian Jews in the early years, as did some elements in the American Jewish communities. But as the urgency of the need became clear, in the early 1880s, such organizations as the French Alliance

Israélite Universelle moved to help migrating Russian Jews. As early as 1881, the Alliance sent Charles Netter to Brody, on the Austrian-Russian border, to help fleeing Jews on their way to America. In December 1881, the Hebrew Emigrant Aid Society (HEAS) was founded. And in April 1882, an international conference was called in Berlin by the German Central Committee for the Russian-Jewish Refugees. This conference set up a full action plan for aiding Russian Jews on their way to Great Britain and North America. The number of Jewish immigrants directly helped by these organizations was relatively small, and most immigrants continued to travel to America on their own. But the organizations' impact was extremely important, for without them governments would have been far less cooperative in allowing Jews to move freely through their territories.

At the great Northern and Western European emigration ports of that period, such as Marseilles, Le Havre, Rotterdam, Southampton, Hamburg, and Bremerhaven, the immigrants found ships for America. Most had shipping line tickets before they left home, while the rest bought them at the ports. The tickets bought at home were usually full "through tickets," which included the railroad trip across Europe, the boat ticket to America, and any necessary tickets to final American destinations. An emigrant from southern Russia might have a railroad ticket from Brody to Marseilles, a boat ticket from Marseilles to New York, and a railroad ticket from New York to Chicago. Arriving in Marseilles, the immigrant might find a boat ready to leave in a day, or might wait for a week or two, meanwhile staying at a hotel or boarding house run by people who spoke her own language, and served *kosher* food—that is, food prepared according to Jewish dietary laws. In some ports, immigrants would stay in areas run by the shipping companies.

Eventually, the immigrant, probably still with the same group that came all the way across Europe together, would find a boat. By the 1880s and 1890s, these were no longer the small sailing ships or the somewhat larger steamships that had earlier taken the German Jews across the Atlantic. Now there were great steamships that could carry hundreds and sometimes even thousands of immigrants on a single voyage. By the 1880s, there were 8,000-ton ships going to North America. By 1897, the 14,350-ton *Kaiser Wilhelm der Grosse*, at that time the largest ocean liner in the world, was regularly making the crossing. By 1906, the 30,000-ton *Mauritania* and *Lusitania* were in the transatlantic service.

The crossing had become much faster, as well. The fastest of these ships regularly crossed the ocean in six to eight days, some of the later ones making the run in just under five days. On the other hand, a great many immigrants were put on far slower and older ships, which often took two to three weeks to make the trip, and sometimes even longer. The immigrants still traveled in steerage, too. A voyage across the North Atlantic in the airless upper cargo hold of even a fast steamship was far from easy. For most, it meant only a somewhat shorter spell of extreme seasickness than earlier immigrants had been forced to endure.

It was a safer crossing than in earlier years, though. And the food was less often spoiled, though it was still usually of very poor quality. Jewish immigrants normally could find ships that had special dietary arrangements, if desired. Since herring was the main dietary staple for all of the immigrants, that mostly meant that Jews had kosher herring and all others just had herring. The taste, the monotony, and the seasickness were about the same.

Russian-Jewish immigrant Leon Solomon, who crossed in 1901, remembers the herring and more:

> The name of the ship was *Kensington*. That ship took ten days to cross the ocean and arrive in the United States. We traveled third class, steerage in the bowels of the ship, and as religious Jews—especially my mother who was ultra pious—we could not partake of the food which the ship provided for us, except herring and potatoes, and hot water or tea. Otherwise we had to subsist on kosher food my mother prepared in advance, to supplement the food which the ocean-going steamer provided for us.
>
> It was a long journey, we suffered from seasickness. I remember how we listened with fear to the steam siren of the ship when it let loose long-powerful blasts, not knowing what the blasts were intended to convey. Whether it was a signal to other ocean-going liners or a warning of some kind, at any rate it was powerful and terrifying.

The cost of crossing the ocean to America came down sharply in those years, which had a lot to do with the volume of immigration to America. Before the First World War, it sometimes cost as little as $10 to $15 to cross the Atlantic in steerage, and never more than $35. Of course, this is not as small an amount as it seems to us today. In 1905, the average American factory wage was about $5 per week, so even $10 was a substantial sum to poor people from Europe. It might take someone years to earn

Steaming past Ellis Island (upper right) and the Statue of Liberty (upper left), the S.S. Imperator is returning to Europe for more immigrants in 1913. The earlier immigration station of Castle Garden is at the lower left.
(Library of Congress)

and put aside enough to be able to bring a family over from Europe.

At the end of the long journey by land and sea was the Mother of Exiles, the great statue that has for a century welcomed immigrants to New York harbor. Polish-Jewish immigrant Arnold Weiss, who arrived in 1921, remembers how it was, seeing the Statue of Liberty for the first time:

> Seeing the Statue of Liberty was the greatest thing I've ever seen. It was really something. What a wonderful sight! To know you're in this country. God, just think of it!
>
> I remember as a child people used to say to me, "In America you'd find gold in the streets." The streets of gold! And as a child I said to myself, "Gee, we're in America. Now I can go out in the streets and pick up gold."

Ellis Island

Then came the last hurdle, the great gateway to America. It was Ellis Island, known all over the world in those times as the Island of Tears. That was understandable. Today, it is seen as an island of hope, through which tens of millions came safely through to America. But to immigrants coming through then, it was the last barrier after the long, hard journey out of Europe and across the ocean. Here is how Fanny Kligerman saw it, arriving with her family in 1905:

> Everybody was sad there. There was not a smile on anybody's face. Here they thought maybe they wouldn't go through. There they thought maybe my child won't go through. There was such a sadness, no smile any place. You could see . . . That's when I came here in 1905. The people had such terrible sad faces. Such a sad place there.
>
> Oh, did I cry. Terribly. When you cry and I can see how you cry, I cry, too. All my sisters and brothers cried. So I cried. You don't know why you cry. Just so much sadness there that you have to cry. But there's more tears in Ellis Island to ten people than, say, to a hundred people elsewhere. There is all of these tears, everybody has tears.

At Ellis Island, it could all come to nothing. You could be sent back to Europe, sick and penniless, if any of a substantial number of things were thought to be wrong with you. You could be sent back for having trachoma (a serious eye disease), favus (a highly contagious scalp disease), tuberculosis, partial blindness or even very poor eyesight, deafness, lameness, and many other reasons. You could even be sent back for general weakness or "mental" problems. All this meant that the immigration inspectors had very wide discretion as to whom to send back. You could be sent back if you said you had a specific job waiting for you—as a threat to the jobs of American workers. You could also be sent back in some periods if you had no money and no prospects of making money. From 1917 on, you could be sent back if you were illiterate, even in your native language. And if a child was sent back to Europe, an adult in the family had to go back, too, breaking up the family. You could also be detained at Ellis

At Ellis Island inspectors "in uniforms like soldiers" checked the eyes of newly landed immigrants.
(Photo by Underwood & Underwood)

Doctors wrote a "K" on the coat of this Russian Jew at Ellis Island in 1905, to indicate that he was to be held for further medical examination.
(Photo by Lewis W. Hine, New York Public Library)

Island while such matters were being settled. For people sent back or detained, Ellis Island was truly an island of tears. For Russian and Eastern European Jews sent back or detained, it was doubly so, for they had no home countries any more. Once out of Russia, especially illegally, there was no going back.

In truth, only a very small percentage of the immigrants were sent back. But there were so many millions of immigrants that even a small percentage added up to tens of thousands of people from the 1800s through the 1920s. In that period, hundreds of thousands more were detained, usually for only a few days, but sometimes for a month or more.

But they came and kept coming, past the Statue of Liberty, past the Ellis Island hurdle, and through the golden door. For most of the Jews arriving in those years, New York City was the end of the journey. For others—and for two-thirds of all the immigrants of that period—the journey went farther on into the country, ending only when they arrived by rail at their destinations. Many Jews went on to join existing Jewish communities in Chicago, Philadelphia, Cincinnati, Boston, San Francisco, and scores of other places in the United States. For some, this was in miles the longest, though by far the easiest, part of the long journey to the new world. In the chapters to come, we will explore the impact of that new world upon the Jews and their impact on it.

5

The Earliest Jewish Immigrants

On August 17, 1790, George Washington visited Newport, Rhode Island. There, the new president was warmly greeted and congratulated by the Jewish community, one of the oldest and most highly respected communities in the new United States. Here is part of his response to those congratulations:

> All possess alike liberty of conscience and immunities of citizenship. It is now no more that toleration is spoken of, as if it was by the indulgence of one class of people, that another enjoyed the exercise of their inherent natural rights. For happily the government of the United States, which gives to bigotry no sanction, to persecution no assistance, requires only that they who live under its protection should demean themselves as good citizens, in giving it on all occasions their effectual support . . .
>
> May the children of the stock of Abraham, who dwell on this land, continue to merit and enjoy the good will of the other inhabitants, while every one shall sit in safety under his own vine and fig tree, and there shall be none to make him afraid.

Washington was talking about very real and present freedom for American Jews in a world which had little of such freedom to offer. Only in France was it possible to look forward to this kind of freedom and equality, and even there it had not yet fully blossomed. A year later, Catherine the Great was to establish the Pale of Jewish Settlement in Russia, while in Central and South America the Inquisition was a very recent memory and anti-Jewish prejudice was still rampant.

Yet freedom was not such a recent thing for American Jews. In America, the idea of freedom for Jews and the idea of freedom for all had been growing side by side for almost two centuries before Washington's speech at Newport. Putting it a little differently, the ideas behind the

Declaration of Independence and the Constitution, with its Bill of Rights, had been growing ever since Pilgrim times—and these ideas meant freedom for Jews, too.

The First Jewish Americans

For those first 23 Jews who landed in New Amsterdam in 1654—and for the two Jews who had preceded them by less than a month—the situation seemed quite different. Indeed, Peter Stuyvesant tried to expel the 23, using the same bigotries they had been encountering in Europe for a thousand years. Stuyvesant failed to expel the Jews, because of the intervention of the Jews of Amsterdam, some of whom were shareholders in the Dutch West India Company.

But for the next 10 years, until British takeover of the colony, Jews had to battle for every bit of equality. In 1655, Jacob Barsimonson and Asser Levy demanded the right to bear arms and serve guard duty, rather than pay a tax. In 1656, the Jews of New Amsterdam won the right to "quietly and peacefully carry on their business . . . and exercise in all quietness their religion within their houses . . ." New Amsterdam's Congregation Shearith Israel, a Spanish-Portuguese Jewish-American congregation, dates from 1656. It was the first Jewish congregation in what was later to become the United States. It was a congregation, rather than a house of worship, because decades were to pass before a house was rented to serve as a synagogue, and it was 1730 before a synagogue was built. Nor was there a rabbi, as such. Rather, a member of the congregation served as reader. Actually, no ordained rabbis settled in the United States until the 1800s. This absence of rabbis, together with the relative "looseness" of the Spanish-Portuguese Jewish religious observance, made it possible for Sephardic (Portuguese) and Ashkenazi (German and other European) Jews to coexist rather easily in the same American congregations.

The small Jewish community in New Amsterdam may have fought for and gained a certain amount of equality, but it did not prosper. New Amsterdam itself did not prosper, becoming increasingly hemmed in by expanding English colonies on both sides. But the situation began to change when the English took the colony from the Dutch in 1664. Then the colony, renamed New York, began to grow, and with it the Jewish community. There were still restrictions, as on the right to open retail shops and the right to vote, but they began to go as the tide of democracy began to rise. By the early 1700s, Jews in New York could and did engage in trades and crafts, and worship as they pleased. At Passover, 1730, New York's Jewish community dedicated the Mill Street Synagogue, the first Jewish house of worship in the colonies. In 1740, the British Parliament passed the Naturalization Act, making it possible for Jews (and other immigrants) to become full citizens of the Colonies after seven years' residence.

New York's Jewish community was small, consisting of a few closely knit families. Most of them were of Spanish-Portuguese origin, such as the Gomez, Luchena, and Pacheco families. Others were of German or other Central European origin, by way of London, such as the families of Moses Levy and Jacob Franks. But their "community" was really much larger than it seemed. For most Jews were merchants and shippers, who were part of a wide set of commercial networks extending from Holland and Great Britain in Europe to the Caribbean and North America. These were not exclusively Jewish trading networks, by any means. But they were part of a much wider world than that of the Colonies. That made it possible for many colonial Jews to prosper as traders by land and sea. Like other such merchants of the time, these colonial Jews traded in such commodities as furs, wheat, tea, lumber, candles, and guns.

They also dealt in slaves, as long as there was a slave trade. People may hunger for freedom, but not necessarily feel the same way about the freedom of others. For that matter, George Washington and Thomas Jefferson held slaves, though with great misgivings. But, misgivings or not, they held slaves. And Jewish sea traders dealt in slaves.

Jews in New England

Although small in number, New York's Jewish community made a vital contribution to American commerce. An equally important and larger Jewish community grew up in Newport, Rhode Island, starting in 1658. By the time of the American Revolution, this community consisted of an estimated 1,000 people, out of 8,000 to 9,000 people in Newport.

Rhode Island had been founded by Roger Williams in 1636. He was a dissenter from narrow Puritanism, and believed in the widest kind of religious toleration and political liberty. The colony he founded reflected his views. When a group of Spanish-Portuguese Jews settled in Newport in 1658, they were welcomed, though with restrictions on their becoming

Many of the earliest Jewish immigrants to America are buried in the cemetery near the Touro Synagogue, which still stands in Newport, Rhode Island.
(Touro Synagogue)

fully naturalized citizens. From then on, the Jewish community grew slowly, buying its own cemetery plot in 1677. After the Naturalization Act of 1740, Newport's Jewish community grew rather quickly, as Jews were attracted to the Colonies in larger numbers, from Europe and the Caribbean. In 1763, the Jews of Newport dedicated their first synagogue—Touro Synagogue—the oldest surviving Jewish house of worship in the United States, today a National Historic Site.

In this period, New England was fast emerging as a great shipping and trading center. The Jews of Newport were part of that development. One, Aaron Lopez, became one of the richest men in the Colonies. He manufactured spermaceti (whale oil) candles, built ships, traded in rum, slaves, and much else, and sent out fleets of whalers. He was also a devout Jew, who in 1759 laid the first of the six cornerstones of the Touro Synagogue. Aaron Lopez had been born a New Christian in Portugal. He had come to Newport from Portugal in 1752, and immediately converted back to Judaism, as had so many of the New Christians (Conversos) as soon as they left Spain and Portugal.

Other Early Jewish Communities

There were three other small but substantial Jewish communities in colonial America, in Savannah, Philadelphia, and Charleston. The Savannah community was short-lived. Starting with the arrival of two groups of Spanish-Portuguese Jews from England in 1733, it had all but disappeared by the 1760s, as Savannah itself nearly failed. But some Jews remained in Savannah and the rest of Georgia, and as the city regained strength in the 1790s, a Jewish community was rebuilt there.

The Philadelphia Jewish community developed in the 1730s, buying a cemetery plot in 1738, and holding religious services from the mid-1740s. By the time of the American Revolution there were many other Jews scattered throughout Pennsylvania, some of Spanish-Portuguese origin and some of German and other Central European origin.

The Charleston Jewish community began to form in the 1690s, but developed very slowly, as a few Jews trickled into the busy port during the early part of the next century. By 1749, a small group of Jews had formed a congregation in Charleston. But South Carolina was far from hospitable to Jews. Here, there was freedom of worship and commerce, but the tendency was to limit, rather than to extend, political rights. Both Catholics and Jews were discriminated against. As late as 1759, the colonial government attempted to bar all but Protestants from political office. Although the British authorities did not allow that to stand, the bigotries present in the South Carolina situation made it far less attractive for Jews than such places as Rhode Island, New York, and Pennsylvania.

There was a good deal of prejudice against Jews in the Colonies, and it was expressed very openly and in many ways. That Jews were freer in North America than anywhere else on earth at the time does not mean that Jews were so very free. Not by modern standards. When George Washington in 1790 spoke of giving "to bigotry no sanction, to persecution no assistance," he was talking about something new in his time. Freedom for Jews had been growing during the colonial period, but it was only after the Revolution that it came to full flower.

Jews in the American Revolution

With the outbreak of the American Revolution came a basic choice of allegiance, for Jews and all other Americans. Some Jews stayed with king and country, making the Loyalist choice. Most, however, went with the Revolution, choosing that course seeming to best lead to political and economic freedom.

It was not an easy decision, nor one dictated simply by economic position in the Colonies. David Franks of New York, part of a wealthy colonial merchant family, was a Loyalist. David S. Franks of Montreal took up the revolutionary cause, retreated with the American occupation troops from Montreal early in the war, and fought out the war on the revolutionary side. Aaron Lopez fled his home in Newport ahead of the invading British fleet and spent the war in Massachusetts. Mordecai Sheftall, a leading merchant of Savannah, helped lead the revolt in that city, and was later captured by the British, along with his son, Sheftall Sheftall.

Scores of Jews took up arms to fight for the Revolution. Young Francis Salvador of South Carolina, son of a London financier, died in battle on August 1, 1776. Colonel Solomon Bush of Philadelphia was wounded after the battle of Brandywine, in 1777, and later captured by the British.

Polish-Jewish immigrant Haym Solomon worked for the cause of the American Revolution in the 1770s.
(Smithsonian Collection of Business Americana)

Benjamin Nones came from France to support the revolutionary cause in 1777 and fought with General Pulaski.

Other Jews worked for the Revolution as well. Haym Solomon, a Polish Jew, was arrested by the British in New York as a probable revolutionary spy in 1776. Then released, he spent two years as a British commissary agent, while actually helping American and French prisoners to escape. In 1778, he was found out and fled to Philadelphia, leaving everything he owned behind. A few years later, in 1781, he became a broker, working to help finance the revolutionary cause. He made money at that kind of work and used some of it to personally finance some of the Continental Congress delegates. James Madison, out of funds and writing to a friend for help, spoke of "The kindness of our little friend in Front Street . . . who obstinately rejects all recompense."

For American Jews, the triumph of the American Revolution was reward enough, and worth far more than any amount of money. Here, finally, was full equality, as expressed in a national Bill of Rights. However, full equality was still not expressed in the laws of many of the states. It would be fought for all during the first half of the 19th century. But the essential point of equality was won with the adoption of the Constitution and its first ten amendments—the Bill of Rights.

There was another kind of equality, though, that was much, much harder to achieve—full social equality, without anti-Jewish prejudice. And this is the kind of equality still being fought for in America, by and for Jews, Blacks, Native Americans, Hispanics, women, and many other discriminated-against groups. Jews were guaranteed equal rights under the Constitution, but much prejudice still endured.

So it was that in 1800, the same Benjamin Nones who had fought with Pulaski in the Revolution was attacked by an anti-Jewish letter in a Philadelphia newspaper, the *Gazette of the United States, and Daily Advertiser*. His response was refused by that newspaper, but was printed by *The Philadelphia Aurora*. Here it is, in part, its words standing on the shoulders of George Washington's letter to the Jews of Newport. Together with the Bill of Rights, these documents sum up the beginning of a new time for Jews in America and in the world.

I *am* a *Jew*. I glory in belonging to that persuasion, which even its opponents, whether Christian, or Mahomedan, allow to be of divine origin—of that persuasion on which Christianity itself was originally

In 1794, forty-five years after Jews founded their first congregation in Charleston, South Carolina, they opened the Beth Elohim Synagogue, later destroyed by fire. (American Jewish Historical Society)

founded, and must ultimately rest—which has preserved its faith secure and undefiled, for near three thousand years—whose votaries have never murdered each other in religious wars, or cherished the theological hatred so general, so unextinguishable among those who revile them. A persuasion, whose patient followers have endured for ages the pious cruelties of Pagans, and of Christians, and persevered in the unoffending practice of their rites and ceremonies, amidst poverties and privations—amidst pains, penalties, confiscations, banishments, tortures, and deaths, beyond the example of any other sect, which the page of history has hitherto recorded.

To be of such a persuasion, is to me no disgrace; though I well understand the inhuman language of bigotted contempt, in which your reporter by attempting to make me ridiculous, as a Jew, has made himself detestable, whatever religious persuasion may be dishonored by his adherence.

But I am a Jew. I am so—and so were Abraham, and Isaac, and Moses and the prophets, and so too were Christ and his apostles . . .

I am a Jew, and if for no other reason, for that reason am I republican . . . Among the nations of Europe we are inhabitants everywhere—but Citizens nowhere *unless in Republics*. Here, in France, and in the Batavian (Dutch) Republic alone, we are treated as men and as brethren. In republics we have *rights*, in monarchies we live but to experience *wrongs*. And why? Because we and our forefathers have *not* sacrificed our principles to our interest, or earned an exemption from pain and poverty, by the deriliction of our religious duties, no wonder we are objects of derision to those, who have no principles, moral or religious, to guide their conduct . . .

Strong words, brave words—the right kind of words at the right time. The Revolution had been won, but the long battle for the new ideas about freedom was just beginning. People like Benjamin Franklin and the leaders of the British Anti-Slavery Society had already begun the fight that would end slavery. A whole new set of attitudes toward equality was developing in the world of George Washington, Benjamin Nones, Thomas Jefferson, and James Madison. In the new United States, after the Revolution, there was a sort of second, quieter revolution in social attitudes.

Even before the Revolution, many Jews and Christians had come together socially, become partners in business, and seen children marry across religious lines. What would have been unthinkable almost

The Mikveh Israel Synagogue on Cherry Street in Philadelphia was dedicated in 1825. (American Jewish Historical Society)

everywhere else in the world was often easily accepted in America. In the early 1740s two of the children of Jacob Franks married Christians, and by the 1790s intermarriage between Jews and Christians was common.

In the 1790s and through the mid-1820s, American Jews became more and more integrated into the life of the new country. Many in the small American Jewish communities made interfaith marriages. Some of these marriages resulted in the conversion of Christians to Judaism, but most either went the other way or resulted in a gradual slipping away from religious observance altogether. By the 1820s, when German and other Central European Jews began to arrive in considerable numbers, the older Spanish-Portuguese Jewish communities were much less important to Jewish-Americans than they had been before the Revolution. But the arrival of the second wave of Jewish immigration changed all that.

6

Immigrants from Germany and Central Europe

Even before the great wave of German-speaking immigrants began to pour into the United States in the 19th century, significant numbers had already arrived. One of the first two Jews in New York, Jacob Barsimonson, was an Ashkenazi—that is, a German-speaker. The Franks family, so prominent in early New York Jewish affairs, was also German-speaking. Indeed, by 1800, an estimated half or more of the small number of Jews in the United States were German-speakers.

Once the great wave of German Jews began to arrive, though, their numbers were overwhelming. Sephardic Jews did remain prominent in American Jewish life. But their numbers were so few that they could not maintain their dominance in the face of this new wave of Jewish immigration. At the time of the American Revolution, there were perhaps 2,000 to 3,000 Jews in the new United States, about half of them Spanish-Portuguese and half German-speaking in origin. By 1840, there were about 15,000 Jews in the United States, the overwhelming majority of them German-speakers. By 1850, the number had jumped to about 50,000; by 1860, to an estimated 150,000. By 1880, when the German-speaking Jewish immigration had slowed greatly, there were an estimated 250,000 to 300,000 Jews in the United States, most of them either German-speakers born in Europe or their children.

Where before the Jews of different origins had coexisted quite peaceably, in the same communities and even in the same religious congregations, now the situation changed. Overwhelmed, the Spanish-Portuguese Jews tended to draw back. On the other hand, the very large numbers of German Jews pressed forward in the New World, transplanting their ideas, religious observances, and German culture. They spread out all over the rapidly expanding United States, bringing religious leaders with them, quickly gaining economic strength, and forming hundreds of new Jewish communities.

In every truly massive migration, there has to be both push and pull. There were certainly powerful reasons pushing German Jews out of Central Europe in those decades. And there were two powerful reasons pulling them to the United States. One was freedom; the other was tremendous economic opportunity.

After winning their independence, Americans began to go west, first in thousands, then in hundreds of thousands, and then in millions. In 1775, Daniel Boone opened the Wilderness Road through Cumberland Gap to Kentucky. By 1820, only 45 years later, there were a million people living in Kentucky and Tennessee. In 1790, there were 45,000 people in Ohio. In 1820, there were over 450,000, 10 times as many. In only 20 years, between 1790 and 1810, 200,000 people moved west through New York's Mohawk Valley to settle the area between Albany and Buffalo.

And that was just the beginning. Immigrants really began pouring into mid-continent in the 1830s. The new United States after the Revolution had a little under 3,000,000 people. By 1860, at the outbreak of the Civil War, there were 31,000,000 people, over 10 times as many, and close to half of them lived in what was then called the West, out beyond the Allegheny Mountains. It was this wonderfully alive America, expanding in all directions, that so attracted the new German-Jewish immigrants.

Making Their Way

Especially in the early years, many German-Jewish immigrants were young single men. Most of them knew hardly any English at first, and had little or no money. Nor were they often skilled craftspeople or farmers, for many such occupations had been barred to them by discrimination in Europe. However, they often did have some business and financial skills, for large numbers of German Jews had for centuries been forced into such despised occupations as peddling and moneylending. They often also had drive and the courage to fight through in personally difficult situations.

What many of them did was to become peddlers, out in the American countryside, around the existing towns and cities and following the frontier westward. In the early days, a young German-Jewish immigrant might work out of New York, Cincinnati, Chicago, Savannah, Montgomery, San Francisco, or any of a score of other cities. He would

Many new immigrants, like this one in about 1850, began in the New World as peddlers, providing necessaries and desirables to people around the country. (Library of Congress)

The earliest Jewish im-migrants prepared the special unleavened bread called matzoh *in their synagogues. By the mid-19th century* matzoh *bread was being made in factories, but still under a rabbi's supervision.*
(Library of Congress)

buy 100 to 200 pounds worth of small, light items—needles, thread, knives, spices, and whatever else country people needed that could easily be carried. Usually the purchase would be made on credit. Then he would go into the countryside, packing it all on his back, walking a circuit for a week or more, until all or most of his goods were sold. Then it would be back to home base, for more goods. It was an extremely difficult life. Peddlers carried their heavy loads in all kinds of weather, slept in fields or barns, and were the prey of any robber who happened to come along. Rabbi Mayer Wise of Cincinnati, himself a German-Jewish immigrant, described the peddlers of the time this way:

> Our people in this country may be divided into the following classes: 1. the basket-peddler—he is as yet altogether dumb and homeless; 2. the trunk-carrier, who stammers some little English, and hopes for better times; 3. the pack-carrier, who carries one hundred to one hundred and fifty pounds upon his back, and indulges the thought that he will become a businessman some day. In addition to these, there is the aristocracy, which may be divided into three classes: 1. the wagon-baron, who peddles through the country with a one- or two-horse team; 2. the jewelry-count, who carries a stock of watches and jewelry in a small trunk, and is considered a rich man even now; 3. the store-prince, who has a shop, and sells goods in it . . . At first one is the slave of the basket or the pack; then the lackey of the horse, in order to become finally the servant of the shop.

For those who were able to make some money at peddling, sooner or later the backpack would indeed become a horse and wagon. Then the horse and wagon would ultimately give way to a store, and one store might become many stores. That was the dream.

For a few, that dream came true. Joseph Seligman went to Mauch Chunk, Pennsylvania, in 1837, became a peddler, and the next year sent for two of his brothers. By 1840, the Seligmans had opened their first store, in Lancaster, Pennsylvania. A year later, they relocated to Mobile, Alabama, and a year after that were able to send for six more family members, followed by the last two one year later. By the early 1850s, they had stores all over the country, and had moved into gold dealing and banking. Later, they were to become the center of a strong, close-knit, mainly German-Jewish financial and social community in New York. That community included, among others, the Lehmans, who had started in America as peddlers and became cotton brokers and bankers; the Guggenheims, who started as peddlers and wound up industrialists and bankers; the Loebs, who started out as textile merchants and became financiers; and a good many more.

But it is possible to make far too much of these kinds of success stories. For every Seligman, there were hundreds of other peddlers who worked at it, failed, and took other low-paying jobs when they could get them. Yet it is also true that as a group, the German Jews had considerable financial success, enough to make most of them solidly middle class and rather prosperous as the 19th century wore on. That general prosperity provided a solid economic base for the many Jewish communities that began to build up all over the country. By the 1850s, every large city had some sort of Jewish community.

Going West

Jews moved west with the American frontier. Joseph Philipson was the first recorded Jew to settle in St. Louis. In 1817, Joseph Jonas founded what was to become the vitally important Jewish community in Cincinnati. There were two Jewish congregations in San Francisco by 1849, the year of the great California Gold Rush. Ed Scheffelin named Tombstone, Arizona. Dodge City had three different Jewish mayors. Jewish traders, peddlers, and merchants were to be found all the way from

Like other Americans in the 19th century, Jews headed westward—all the way to California, where A. Levi ran a store and livery stable. (San Diego Historical Society)

the Appalachians to the Pacific. So were Jewish teachers, preachers, scouts, politicians, gamblers, and horsethieves.

Many of the young, single men who formed the bulk of the early German-Jewish immigration never did rejoin organized Jewish communities in the New World. Often, they married women of other faiths and ethnic groups, including Native Americans and Blacks, and made no serious attempt to practice Judaism or to become a part of non-religious Jewish groups. Most German Jews, however, did develop communities, in the religious as well as the ethnic sense. By the mid-1850s, there were over 100 Jewish congregations in the United States. Many of them were led by ordained rabbis who had emigrated from the German-speaking countries. These rabbis carried far more religious weight than had the lay readers of the earlier Spanish-Portuguese synagogues, and soon came to dominate American Jewish religious life and institutions. The Judaism they developed in America was in some ways quite different from the Orthodox Judaism practiced by some German-speaking Jews and by the vast majority of the Eastern European Jews who later came to America.

Reform Judaism

What developed in America was Reform Judaism, which was in essence a movement to modernize Jewish religious practice without losing the Jewish faith.

The movement toward a modernized Judaism had started on both sides of the Atlantic after the American and French revolutions. As Jews moved fully out into the national mainstream, many left Judaism to become non-religious freethinkers. Many of these freethinkers still thought of themselves as Jews, as have large numbers of Jews in every generation since then. Other Jews converted to Christianity. Most, however, held fast to their faith, either in its existing form or by trying to change its practices to—as they saw it—make it better suited to modern times.

The center of the European Reform Jewish movement was Germany. There, even before the French Revolution, some of the basic ideas that would lead to the Reform movement were being propounded by Moses Mendelssohn and those around him. They continued to do so through the early 1800s. In 1819, they formed the first major Reform Jewish organization, the Association for Jewish Culture and Knowledge—and began to fully develop Reform Judaism.

In the new United States, there was no such formal early development, for there were no rabbis and very few intellectuals to carry such thinking into practice. There were, however, movements toward modernization. The most notable of these was at Temple Beth Elohim, Charleston, South Carolina, in 1824. There, a group of young Sephardic Jews, much influenced by German Reform Jewish thinking, established the Reform Society of Israelites. They demanded such changes in traditional practices as family pews, rather than segregation of men and women; shorter services; and a choir that included women. But these and other seemingly small changes split the congregation, and started a battle that lasted 20 years. That battle was never really settled, just as the differences between the Reform, Orthodox, and Conservative versions of Judaism have never been settled to this day.

In the emerging American German-Jewish community, however, Reform Judaism did become by far the strongest influence. That was so from the 1840s until large numbers of Orthodox Jews began arriving from Eastern Europe in the 1880s.

In the 1840s, several Reform rabbis who were to become very influential began to arrive in the United States. These included David Einhorn, the intellectual leader of Reform Judaism in America, known as a radical reformer in his day. His essential ideas were carried forward to become the main platform of American Reform Judaism, under the leadership of his son-in-law, Kaufmann Kohler.

Such well-known rabbis as Isaac Mayer Wise, Max Lilienthal, Leo Merzbacher, and Samuel Adler arrived in that period, as well. Samuel Adler became Rabbi of Temple Emanuel of New York. His son, Felix Adler, was trained to be a rabbi, but left Judaism to found the Ethical Culture Society, a non-religious organization.

During the next 40 years, the ideas of these rabbis were to carry Reform Judaism far beyond its German origins. The concepts were opposed in their time by the thinking of a much smaller, conservative American Jewish group, led by Isaac Leeser, editor of the *Occident*. But the opposition was unable to prevail against the tide of Reform.

Isaac Mayer Wise was the main leader of Reform Judaism in the United States. He had emigrated from Germany with his wife and daughter in 1846, when he was 27 years old, and soon became rabbi of Congregation Beth El, in Albany, New York. In 1854, he became rabbi of Congrega-

*Rabbi Isaac Mayer Wise
led the late-19th-century
movement for Reform
Judaism from his base in
Cincinnati.*
(American Jewish
Archives)

The richness and grandeur of the Temple Emanu-El at Fifth Avenue and 43rd Street in New York City, at its dedication in 1868, testified to the prosperity of at least some portions of the German Jewish community.
(Library of Congress)

tion B'nai Jeshurun, in Cincinnati, Ohio. In 1855, Reform rabbi Max Lilienthal became rabbi of a neighboring congregation, B'nai Israel.

From the 1850s on, Reform Judaism began to take form as the leading American Jewish religious belief and organization. In 1854, Wise founded the *Israelite*, later the *American Israelite*, an English-language weekly. Soon after, he founded *Die Deborah*, a German-language weekly. In 1855, he called together the first national conference of American Reform rabbis. In 1857, he published German and English editions of a new prayer book, *Minhag America (The American Way)*. In 1873, he was prime mover in the formation of the Reform Jewish Union of American Hebrew Congregations. In 1875, he founded Cincinnati's Hebrew Union College.

The German-Jewish-American community was overwhelmingly in favor of Reform Judaism. Yet not all of the Reformers were agreed that full Americanization was the way. David Einhorn, for example, would preach to his congregation only in German, and viewed Americanization with great distrust. But Wise, Lilienthal, and the other Americanizers triumphed.

Community Organizations

As a large Jewish-American community began to emerge, so did many community organizations, some of them becoming national and even international in scope. By the 1830s, American Jews were beginning to create a huge web of fraternal orders, benevolent societies, burial societies, social clubs, literary societies, immigrant aid societies, and educational institutions. In this, they were like most other substantial immigrant groups, who generally created both religious and nonreligious organizations as they built American communities.

The first national Jewish fraternal order was the B'nai B'rith (Children of the Covenant), which was organized in New York City in 1843. It soon began to grow tremendously, establishing itself in many American communities, and later internationally, as well. In 1913, it organized its Anti-Defamation League, an action arm devoted to battling anti-Semitism. Starting in the 1850s, Jewish orphanages and hospitals began to be established throughout the country. Later in the century, German-Jewish-American organizations were to be extremely active in creating a wide range of immigrant aid organizations. Some, such as the Hebrew Emigrant Aid Society (HEAS), and the later Hebrew Immigrant Aid Society (HIAS), helped Jews on their way across Europe and through their arrival in America. Others, such as the Educational Alliance, helped new immigrants as they made their way into a new language and culture.

Many German Jews also participated freely in the life of the German-American community, through personal and business friendships and through membership in a wide range of German-American organizations. The wider German-American community was also in those years creating large numbers of social, cultural, and educational organizations, and Jews were very much a part of them. This reflected growing democracy in Germany as well as in the United States. And after the German democratic revolutions of 1848, small but very influential groups of liberal Germans began to immigrate, bringing their views of equality with them. These were often people who viewed equality for Jews as a matter of principle, and extended that feeling to all people, including Black slaves. Some of them were to be active in the antislavery cause, before and during the Civil War.

Jews and the Civil War

It was around the question of slavery that the greatest differences were to develop among American Jews. Although the great majority of American Jews had been for the Revolution, their allegiances were far more divided as the issue of slavery began to split the nation. There were many Jews on both sides of the issue, before and during the Civil War.

To some extent, it was a question of where people lived. When it came to actual war, Northern Jews tended to support the Union, while Southern Jews tended to support the Confederacy. But the issue of slavery had begun to divide the country long before the Civil War; by the 1840s there were both Southern Jewish abolitionists and Northern Jews in favor of slavery. For example, Rabbi Isaac Mayer Wise of Cincinnati called Blacks "debased and inferior," and called abolitionists "demons of death and destruction." But Rabbi David Einhorn of Baltimore was an ardent abolitionist, who called slavery a "rebellion against God," and wrote: "Break the bonds of oppression, let the oppressed go free and tear every yoke!" Like other abolitionists, Einhorn was attacked by pro-slavery forces

Louisiana Senator Judah P. Benjamin became secretary of war and then secretary of state for the Confederacy during the Civil War. His face appeared on Confederate war bonds and on the two-dollar bill. (Library of Congress)

Dr. Jacob Da Silva Solis-Cohen served the Union Army as acting fleet surgeon in the squadron enforcing the blockade of the South.
(American Jewish Archives)

before the Civil War. He fled his home in Baltimore in 1861, but lived to see the Civil War settle the matter.

There were many other Jewish abolitionists as well, such as Ernestine Rose, who fought for abolition of slavery and at the same time for women's rights, and August Bondi, who fought beside John Brown in Kansas against proslavery forces. There were many strong Jewish supporters of slavery in the South, such as Judah P. Benjamin, Senator from Louisiana. But although many Jews took opposing sides on slavery, the great majority took no strong position at all, until the outbreak of the Civil War. Then, like all Americans, they took sides and fought for the Union or the Confederacy. An estimated 10,000 Jews served in armies and thousands more were involved in the war efforts of each side. In the Confederacy, for example, Judah P. Benjamin became secretary of war and then secretary of state, while David De Leon became surgeon general. The Union army listed four Jewish generals, scores of officers, and thousands of enlisted men.

Similarly, Jews were active in the provisioning and financing of both war efforts. The Seligmans supplied uniforms to the Union army and sold Federal bonds abroad; Joseph Seligman himself was a guest at Abraham Lincoln's table. The Lehmans continued their cotton business in Alabama, sold Confederate bonds abroad, and were close to leading people in the Confederacy. But this kind of work also made money, and brought charges of profiteering in both the Union and the Confederacy. General Ulysses S. Grant's General Order Number 11, in December 1862, ordered the evacuation of all Jews from the Tennessee Department, which he commanded. Abraham Lincoln reversed the order as soon as he learned of it, but the order did cause great concern among Jews in the Union. Yet profiteering and charges of profiteering are part of every war—to be forgotten soon afterwards. Interestingly enough, during the presidency of Ulysses S. Grant, peacetime profiteering and corruption flourished at least as much as they had during the war years.

After the war, the country grew by leaps and bounds, and so did the security and prosperity of its Jewish-American communities. A new Jewish merchant and banking elite arose centered in New York. Strong national religious and community organizations developed. The swing from German-based to English-based language and culture accelerated, as both the German and the German-Jewish communities further merged

Jewish-Americans celebrated their own holidays; here they observe Purim, on March 14, 1865, with a costume ball in New York City.
(Library of Congress)

with the larger American community. And so it stood in the early 1880s, when large numbers of Russian and other Eastern European Jews began to arrive in the United States, changing everything.

Charles M. Strauss, born in Boston, was elected mayor of Tucson, Arizona, in 1883, a few years after this photograph was taken. (Arizona Historical Society)

7

The Eastern European Jews

Right on the face of it, there were tremendous differences between the masses of Eastern European Jews who began to arrive in the 1880s and the earlier Spanish-Portuguese and German-Jewish Americans. The notable thing was that all got along as well as they did, rather than that there were abrasions among the groups. Their Old World languages were different, their cultures were different, their religious practices were different, where and how they lived on arrival were different, and their politics were different. In America, even their classes were different, at least at the start, for German Jews were the chief employers in the garment industry, and Eastern Europeans were the chief—and greatly exploited—workers in that industry.

More than that, the German Jews had come as part of a huge German immigration that spread over the whole country. The new immigrants came as a separate people and settled in tight city communities, especially New York City. Many German Jews regarded the newcomers as uncouth foreigners—coarse, pushy paupers who were a source of embarrassment and a heavy moral and financial obligation. Many Eastern European Jews regarded the German Jews as smug hypocrites, exploitive bosses, and turncoats who had given away their ethnic heritage and religion for the sake of a kind of contemptuous half-acceptance by the Christian world.

Yet ultimately they got on together. In the early years, the German Jews helped the newcomers a great deal. Their organizations helped Russian and Rumanian Jews flee Europe and travel all the way across the Atlantic, through Castle Garden and later Ellis Island. Their political influence and money helped smooth the way in the new country. Some of their best young people, like nurse Lillian Wald, set up organizations like the Henry Street Settlement, which helped raise health and living standards tremendously. Some of the most socially minded wealthy German Jews, like Jacob Schiff, helped fund educational organizations of great and lasting value, such as the Educational Alliance. Perhaps, as some said, the German Jews helped so much mostly because they wanted to Americanize those embarrassing "Russian" Jews as fast as possible. Perhaps—and this is much closer to the truth—it was more a matter of simple humanity, and their own Jewish identity, to help other Jews fleeing Czarist oppression.

Both the Henry Street Settlement and the Educational Alliance were on New York's Lower East Side, cradle of the new Jewish immigration. After coming through Castle Garden or, later, Ellis Island, a few of the new Jewish immigrants went on to Boston, Philadelphia, Chicago, Cincinnati, Minneapolis, San Francisco, and the other Jewish communities around the country. But the great majority went no farther than a short walk north through the financial district to the Lower East Side. There, they became part of what would soon become a community of well over a million New York Jews. From the time of that first Jewish landing in New Amsterdam back in 1654, New York City had always been one of the main centers of Jewish population in the United States. Now, the sheer mass of this new Jewish immigration quickly made it the largest concentration of Jews in the world.

Many German-Jewish-Americans, such as Lillian Wald, shown here in about 1910, worked hard to ease the way for later Jewish immigrants from Eastern Europe.
(Library of Congress)

Children like this 12-year-old boy worked alongside adults in dirty, crowded, tenement firetraps called "sweatshops." (Photo by Jacob Riis, about 1889, Library of Congress)

The New Immigrants

For most of these new Jewish immigrants, the change was enormous. It was, as for so many other immigrants, a whole change of language and culture. But it was even more, for most of these people were going from small villages and country places into huge cities, and from village crafts into factories. But not all; a small minority of the Eastern European Jews came from such large cities as St. Petersburg, Kiev, Odessa, and Warsaw. For most, though, the life of the factories and the narrow, dirty city streets felt in some ways far worse than what they had left behind. Yet the great majority stayed on, for freedom and economic opportunity far outweighed the negative side.

What most of them eventually did was to organize unions to fight for better wages and working conditions, develop political strength, create new health, welfare, and self-educational activities, and go into their own businesses to become independent. They also sent their children to school, to freely become all kinds of professionals. So within two generations there were Eastern European Jewish teachers, writers, social workers, doctors, dentists, lawyers, politicians, managers, and a great deal more, in every state of the Union.

In the large cities where they settled, Eastern European Jews often established open-air markets like this one on Maxwell Street in Chicago in about 1905. (Chicago Historical Society, Barnes-Crosby No. 155)

These immigrants found a much more settled United States than the German Jews who had started arriving in the 1830s. Some became peddlers and then storekeepers, as had the German Jews, but relatively few. Those who did become peddlers often did so right in the major cities, going from door to door and street to street. A few of them kept at it, and eventually developed larger-scale junk businesses. But most peddlers soon went on to other retail businesses or into work for wages.

Others of these new immigrants went directly into businesses, usually retail, by working for others, often later to work for themselves. For example, you might in any New York neighborhood of the 1930s find a candy, clothing, or food store run by people of Eastern European Jewish origin.

Most, however, went to work for wages, usually in the garment industry, but also as butchers, house painters, furriers, cigar makers, and even in heavy industry, though in smaller numbers.

Especially in New York City, but also in Chicago and Philadelphia, large numbers of immigrant Jews went into the garment industry. Many in the 1880s and 1890s started as home contractors, being paid miserably little, and by the piece, with the whole family, including the very small children, working as much as 16 hours a day, seven days a week, to make ends meet. However, as new labor laws made it more difficult to exploit home workers and especially children, the work moved more and more into factories. These were for the most part the small, crowded, dirty, unventilated places so aptly called "sweatshops." The name has stuck. To this day, the same kinds of places now employing Spanish-speaking and East Asian immigrants, are still properly called sweatshops.

Bread and Roses

In the 1880s and 1890s, American labor was beginning to organize, and soon enough the immigrant garment workers were doing the same. They had an advantage, in a way, for by the early 1900s veteran socialist and anarchist organizers, who had come to America along with everybody else, were working in the garment and other industries.

In 1884, and again in 1886, there were cloakmakers' strikes. The 1886 strike resulted in the formation of the Cloakmakers Benevolent Association. In 1888, with Socialist leadership, the United Hebrew Trades labor organization was founded. By 1890, it had many affiliates, going far beyond the garment trades and including bakers, painters, musicians, actors, and more. In 1901, a capmakers union was formed; in 1902, a furriers union; and in 1903, the International Ladies Garment Workers Union (ILGWU). None of these unions was very large or strong. The largest was the ILGWU, and that had at most 10,000 members in those years. But starting in 1909, a series of major strikes changed the situation.

On November 22, 1909, after years of exploitation, including a great deal of sexual discrimination, and several small, mostly unsuccessful strikes, a union meeting at Cooper Union, in New York City, attracted thousands of young women garment workers. After hours and hours of speeches and talk, the problems faced by the tens of thousands of young women in the shirtwaist industry seemed no closer to solution. Finally, a striking teenager named Clara Lemlich stood up in the hall and made an impassioned speech, in Yiddish, that took the meeting by surprise—and by storm. She said:

> I am a working girl, one of those striking against intolerable conditions. I am tired of listening to speakers who talk in generalities. What we are here for is to decide whether or not to strike. I offer a resolution that a general strike be declared—now!

And so it was, by thousands of young Jewish women, finally taking the oath: "If I turn traitor to the cause I now pledge, may this hand wither from the arm I raise!"

The resultant strike of 20,000 young women shirtwaist workers, about two-thirds of them Jewish and most of the rest of them Italian, made American labor history, American Jewish history, and American Italian history. The strike drew a great deal of attention, getting support from social workers like Lillian Wald and society women like Anne Morgan, J.P. Morgan's daughter. It lasted almost three months, and brought only partial victory, but it demonstrated that labor unions were becoming a force to be reckoned with. And with more powerful unions came social reform.

The women had led the way. On July 7, 1910, 60,000 cloakmakers went on strike, and by September had won a major victory. The same year,

Young Jewish immigrant women like this one spearheaded strikes that led to unionization in the garment industry. (Photo by Lewis W. Hine, New York Public Library)

the long Hart, Schaffner, and Marx strike in Chicago began what would later become the Amalgamated Clothing Workers of America union.

But the shirtwaist industry was to provide another kind of milestone, as well. On March 25, 1911, at the Triangle Shirtwaist Company in New York City, 146 people, most of them young Jewish and Italian women, died by fire. The building was a firetrap; and the exit doors had been locked by the company so that no one could slip out on company time. There had been demands for better laws to protect working people in New York, but no one had listened. Here is how union leader Rose Schneiderman, speaking at a public meeting, saw it:

> I would be a traitor to these poor burned bodies if I came here to talk good fellowship. We have tried you good people of the public and we have found you wanting. The old Inquisition had its rack and its thumbscrews and its instruments of torture with iron teeth. We know what these things are today; the iron teeth are our necessities, the thumbscrews are the highpowered and swift machinery close to which we must work, and the rack is here in the firetrap structures that will destroy us the minute they catch on fire.
>
> This is not the first time girls have been burned alive in the city. Every week I must learn of the untimely death of one of my sister workers. Every year thousands of us are maimed. The life of men and women is so cheap and property is so sacred . . .
>
> I can't talk fellowship to you who are gathered here. Too much blood has been spilled. I know from my experience it is up to the working people to save themselves . . .

Rose Schneiderman was right enough about what had gone before. But after the Triangle Fire, reform-minded New Yorkers joined labor to create a set of model factory safety laws, which were enforced and which prevented other such tragedies from happening.

In a single generation, the Eastern European Jews of the great wave of Jewish immigration had created a whole new world of work and organization in America. They had organized, won the right to have unions, and seen protective legislation enacted.

Community Organizations

They also created a whole body of their own health and welfare organizations. The earliest and most basic of these were the mutual aid societies, formed of people from their own, original towns in Eastern Europe, and called *landsmannschaften*. These societies were especially important in New York City, where substantial groups of people from the same hometowns in Europe lived close by each other. The mutual benefit societies supplied such important services as medical care, credit when needed, funeral and burial arrangements, and insurance. Often, they also provided vitally important job leads, through fellow members. And they were a place to go, a kind of social center around which life could revolve in an alien land. Later, when people began to move away, these *landsmannschaften* lost much of their importance as community centers, but were still maintained as a last link with a bygone life (and also as a source of some long-term benefits).

More widely based fraternal societies also developed. Many of the smaller early mutual aid societies merged into larger societies, some of them national. The national Workmen's Circle organization, for example, had 50,000 members in the early 1900s, years before the unions gained similar strength.

Political Action

Eastern European Jews tended to become politically aware and involved in American politics very quickly. Perhaps that was mostly because the experience of freedom was such a treasured thing. Perhaps, also, it was because there were such strong labor union and radical political currents at work on the Lower East Side of New York. Perhaps it was also a matter of finding such currents at work in the larger American community. There was a strong anarchist movement in the United States before the European Jews arrived, and the mostly anarchist Industrial Workers of the World (IWW) organization was active and strong in the West while the Eastern European Jews were still arriving on the East Coast. There was a strong socialist movement in the United States, of which the Jewish Socialist movement was only a small part. Eugene V. Debs secured over 900,000 votes running on the Socialist Party ticket in 1912.

Among the immigrant radicals deported just after World War I was Russian Jewish anarchist Emma Goldman. (American Museum of Immigration, Statue of Liberty National Monument, National Park Service, U.S. Department of the Interior, Sherman Collection)

Of the two main radical currents of the time, anarchism and socialism, socialism was by far the strongest among Eastern European Jewish immigrants. There were, however, some anarchists among the immigrants, and some who adopted anarchism while in the United States. Anarchists basically believed that all governments, of any kind, were undesirable and should be abolished. Socialists basically believed that all means of producing wealth should be owned by the government. Some socialists believed that governments should be run by special groups, usually meaning themselves.

One of the best-known anarchists in the country was Emma Goldman, who came to Rochester, New York, from Russia in 1886, at the age of 17. She was an active anarchist by the time she was 20, and by 1906 was coediting the well-known anarchist newspaper, *Mother Earth*, with Alexander Berkman. She had met and become Berkman's companion back in Rochester. He was the anarchist who shot and wounded industrialist Henry Clay Frick during the Homestead Steel strike of 1892, and served 14 years in jail for it. Goldman and Berkman were active anarchists in the United States until 1917, when they were both arrested for opposing the draft. In 1919, they were both deported to Russia. Neither stayed there, though, for Soviet communism turned out to be far from what either had in mind. He died in Europe in 1936. She died in Canada in 1940.

But anarchism never came to much among American Jews, who were too busy making a new, freer life to want to spend much time taking down the democratic government of their new country. The entirely false portrait of the bomb-throwing, anarchist Jew with a big, black, bushy beard was, however, much favored by the press and American bigots. This kind of fiction was used for decades by those who wanted to end immigration and stir up anti-Semitism in the United States.

The movement that did gain considerable strength among America's Eastern European Jews was socialism. A few had brought a belief in some sort of Socialist solution to the world's ills along with them from Eastern Europe. Most became socialists in the United States, as part of the large American socialist movement of the time.

The strength of socialism lay mostly in the trade unions, rather than in politics. During this period, only one Socialist, Meyer London, was elected to Congress from New York City's 9th Congressional District on the East Side. Only one Socialist, Morris Hillquit, made a serious attempt at the New York mayoralty. He never was able to win the office. There were many Socialists in other state and city offices, after the election of 1912, in which Hillquit ran strongly, but they did not last long in office. The leaders of the garment workers unions were Socialists, however, and most remained so all their lives, even though they became part of Franklin Roosevelt's New Deal Democratic coalition in the 1930s, and have generally stayed with the Democrats ever since.

As is true of all ethnic groups in the United States, the main electoral choice was to vote and become active in the Republican or Democratic parties. Many Eastern European American Jews voted Socialist before the First World War, but most voted for the Republican Party of Abraham Lincoln and Theodore Roosevelt, as had the German Jews before them. That was partly because reformers tended to be Republicans in Irish Democratic-controlled New York City politics. It was also because Theodore Roosevelt was much beloved of large numbers of New York Jews, as a New York reformer and a leader who had always treated them with careful courtesy. It was only with the Crash of 1929, the Depression, and the election of Franklin D. Roosevelt in 1932 that most American Jews became, and stayed, Democrats.

New Jewish Communities

In New York, as in other cities with substantial numbers of Eastern European Jews, tight Jewish ethnic communities formed. These have often been called ghettos, but that is not what they were. In many places, Jews faced discrimination if they moved outside the early Jewish community, but they faced no legal restrictions, as in medieval Europe or Nazi Germany. In the United States, even the great wave of Eastern European Jewish immigrants experienced far less discrimination than Black Americans, Native Americans, Asian Americans, or, in some places, Spanish-speaking Americans.

People in the early Jewish communities began to move outward as soon as they made a little money. In New York, it was out to the Williamsburg and Brownsville sections of Brooklyn, as soon as the Brooklyn Bridge made that easier. Later, it was to Harlem and the Bronx, and then out to all the New York suburbs. The pattern was repeated in cities everywhere, as it was for all ethnic groups. And as with all ethnic groups, people tended to create new ethnic communities when they moved, rather than to simply

This Lower East Side synagogue, where worshipers celebrated the Jewish New Year in September 1907, is far different from the rich German-Jewish synagogue on New York's Fifth Avenue. (Library of Congress, Bain Collection)

Though most Jewish im-migrants lived in cities, some settled on the land, like those who displayed their products in the Jewish Farmers of America exhibition in October 1909. (Library of Congress, Bain Collection)

merge with the larger population, for America is more a mosaic than a melting pot.

These early ethnic communities had a whole host of supportive people and institutions, by no means all of them ethnic. In the Jewish communities, for example, there were the Jewish mutual aid societies, the Jewish settlement houses and educational institutions, the Jewish synagogues, and the largely Jewish labor and political organizations. But the main schools were American, and taught in English. The government and the law were American, and were administered by English-speaking people. All professions but the religious ones were conducted in English. Therefore, and quite obviously, the main way up and out for poor people was education and mastery of the ways of the new English-speaking world in which they found themselves.

Education and Self-Education

For the People of the Book, education and self-education proved no great problem. They were helped enormously by having a free public elementary and high school system, and an excellent free public library system. In New York, they even had a free public college system, which for poor people, including tens of thousands of Jews, proved a lifelong blessing. Very often it was hard to support yourself through college, especially for women, who were expected to go to work or marry right after high school. But for women and men who really wanted to go to college, it was there and free, whether as a free four-year college or as night college, which might take as long as 10 years. People all over the world thought that in America you could start out poor and uneducated and wind up as a college president or Supreme Court justice. It was so; with education you could do it. And if you couldn't do it yourself, then your children and their children could.

For children, the process of acquiring an American education was plainly set out. Schooling was required by law, and if you were going to attend an American school taught solely in English, you had to know English. One Jewish immigrant remembers arriving at the age of 10, knowing no English:

> Since I arrived in July, I had approximately six weeks to pick up some English . . . After Labor Day, I registered in a public school on Delancey and Ludlow Streets and was put into a special class for foreigners. They called it, I think, the C Class. After being there for about two months, they put me into 4B which I think was the class corresponding to my age level. From there on I went through the fifth year and the sixth year and then I entered Junior High School 20 on Livingston and Forsyth Streets. I guess I was a good student because I was put into rapid advance classes . . . which meant that I made the seventh and eighth year in one year and the ninth year in the second year.

He graduated from junior high at the age of 14, and went to work. At the same time, while working full-time, he took three more years at night high school to get his diploma, and then went on to night college for seven more years and graduated. All that took enormous strength and perseverance, but it was not an unusual story in those days. These were people who were out to make all they could of what the country had to offer.

Another immigrant child remembers the free library system:

> I was an avid reader. The kids I was with in P.S. 64 were always placed in alphabetical order, so Fine came before Finkel and Fisher came after Fine. Fine, Finkel, and Fisher became fast friends, and we used to make a tour of libraries. You could take out only two books from each library, but if you went to enough libraries, you could get during the week as many as six or eight books. I read everything . . . .

That same child later went on to Townsend Harris High School, one of the best schools of its day, and free. Then on to college and out into the world as a highly qualified professional.

Another immigrant child did it a little differently. He went to a religious-based elementary school—a *yeshiva*—in New York, but then on to Townsend Harris and college. He remembers City College as a "tough" school, with a demanding faculty. But he went on through, and became one of the greatest rabbis of his day.

For adults, education was a matter of surviving and moving ahead in a new world. Hundreds of thousands of immigrant Jews went to night school out of a very basic need to learn the language of their new country. To become a citizen, to get and hold a decent job, to do any of a dozen other major and necessary things, you had to have the language of the country. Adults also went to trade schools, technical schools, and night high schools and colleges, studying everything from American history to plumbing. The great immigrant years were also years that saw a tremendous adult education movement in the United States.

Religious Life

Many of the new Jewish immigrants brought with them a strongly orthodox version of Judaism. All of life centered around their religion, and all of that religion was devoted to a study of traditional Jewish law and practice. Every member of every congregation knew the Hebrew texts by heart, and services were conducted wholly in Yiddish, rather than in the languages of any of the countries from which they came. Not all of the new Jewish immigrants brought along this religion, of course, for at that time there were strong nonreligious movements among Jews in Eastern Europe, such as socialism, Zionism, and anarchism, and also a widespread move to a belief, called rationalism, that human reason should be the center of life and living.

Orthodox Judaism conflicted very sharply with established Reform Judaism. The new immigrant would have little of Reform. In the early years, and often later as well, most of those who could not accept Orthodox Judaism left religious belief altogether. Others, who had been Orthodox in Europe, found themselves leaving Orthodoxy and the practice of Judaism under new American conditions. It proved very hard to continue to center life around a religion and set of religious practices, while at the same time learning English, going to night school, and becoming deeply involved in a whole new country and culture.

Yet, by the beginning of World War I, in 1914, there were ten times as many new American Jews from Eastern Europe as there had been American Jews before they came; even though many soon left Orthodoxy, there were still more American Orthodox than Reform Jews in the early part of this century. Orthodoxy was also concentrated in New York and a few other big cities, making it possible to maintain closely knit religious communities among the first generation of immigrants, and to some extent on into the second generation (children born in this country).

At the same time, a third version of Judaism developed. This was Conservative Judaism, which had started as an extension of the earlier battle between reform-minded German American Jews led by Isaac Mayer Wise and some of the earlier Orthodox Jews led by Isaac Leeser. By 1887, a group of Conservative-minded synagogues had started the Jewish Theological Seminary, in New York City. By the turn of the century, some of the Conservatives had gone back to Reform Judaism. But the coming of the Eastern European Jews opened new possibilities to them. In the early years of this century, Conservative Judaism began to grow. In our time, Conservative Judaism has become the largest of the three branches of American Judaism. Today, about 50% of those identifying themselves as believing Jews are Conservative, while about 40% are Reform and 10% Orthodox.

Boris Thomashefsky was but one of many actors playing in the popular American Yiddish theater in the early 20th century.
(American Jewish Historical Society)

Jewish Culture

Much of what holds a large, tightly knit immigrant community together is its own press and its own culture. In the case of the new Jewish community, there was much of both.

By 1900, there were scores of Yiddish newspapers in the United States, most of them small weeklies devoted to community news. Some socialist papers had also emerged, but these too were relatively small in circulation and influence. In New York, however, a substantial newspaper had grown, the *Yidisher Tageblatt*, which claimed a circulation by 1900 of about 100,000. It was a rather conservative popular newspaper, and much like the other lively, untruthful New York papers of the day. The only difference was that it was in Yiddish and concerned itself with matters of interest to its Jewish readers.

New York's socialists decided to compete. The socialist *Jewish Daily Forward*, edited by Abraham Cahan, started publication on April 22, 1897, and soon became by far the most influential Jewish newspaper in the country. It became, in fact, much more than a socialist newspaper as the years went by, for it reported on matters that meant a great deal to its immigrant readers and went far beyond narrow partisan politics. But its most notable contribution was to bring its own readers into the newspaper. In 1906, the *Forward* developed the *Bintel Briefs* (*Bundle of Letters*), in which its readers wrote to the paper about their whole range of problems and hopes, and responded to each others' letters, as well.

There were many writers in the new Jewish communities, almost all of them writing in Yiddish, rather than English. Few of them were translated into English. Some wrote for the *Forward*, the *Tageblatt*, and other newspapers. Most led the hand-to-mouth existence of so many writers, then and now, working at other occupations while stealing as much time as possible for their writing. In the 1890s, such poets as David Edelstadt, Morris Winchevsky, and Morris Rosenfeld began the short period in which Yiddish writers flourished in America. In the next 20 years, they were joined by such writers as Mani Lieg, Moshe Halpern, and Abraham Reisen. In 1914, they were joined by the great Jewish writer Sholom Aleichem, but for only a little while. He died in New York in 1916. Tens of thousands came to mourn.

There was also the Yiddish theater. It has survived in a limited form to this day. But in those times, it was a major force in Jewish cultural life. Through the Yiddish theater, immigrant Jews were able to see the greatest plays of the age, some written directly in Yiddish, and others translated into Yiddish. The works of such Yiddish playwrights as Sholom Aleichem, I.L. Peretz, Sholem Asch, and Leon Kobrin found large audiences. So did the works of Shakespeare, Ibsen, and many of the other great playwrights of the European world. There were great theater companies, such as Maurice Schwartz' Yiddish Art Theater. One of its stars was Muni Weisenfreund, known later in Hollywood as Paul Muni. There were great actors and actresses—Jacob Adler, Molly Picon, Zelig Mogulesco, and Bertha Kalish, to name just a few. Most of all there was life and vitality, and a great upsurge of Jewish talent and creativity that enriched the entire national Jewish community.

There were other artists as well—painters, sculptors, and graphic artists like Ben Shahn, William Zorach, Jacob Epstein, Jo Davidson, and scores of others, who started in such immigrant communities as the Lower East Side and later moved into the mainstream of American art and culture.

And last but far from least, there were the great popular entertainers, who started their national and world careers in those Jewish communities. Irving Berlin, Fannie Brice, Al Jolson, Sophie Tucker, Eddie Cantor, George Burns, Milton Berle, and hundreds of others came out of the Lower East Side in New York and from other American Jewish communities—and went right into the mainstream of the American experience.

It is to that mainstream that we now turn, and to the story of how these Jewish emigrants from Eastern Europe became part of the whole American mosaic.

8

Into the Mainstream

By the 1920s and 1930s, the new Jewish emigrants from Eastern Europe were moving into the mainstream of American life. By then, Al Jolson was America's first talking movie star—the world-renowned *Jazz Singer*. Fannie Brice had graduated from the Lower East Side to become a Ziegfeld Follies star, and then radio's Baby Snooks. Jack Benny, Eddie Cantor, and George Burns, who had by then teamed up with Gracie Allen, were America's best-known radio stars. The music of Irving Berlin, George Gershwin, and Jerome Kern was part of the fabric of the times, and the writers themselves were national institutions. So were such popular jazz musicians as Benny Goodman and Artie Shaw. The Marx Brothers were among the greatest movie stars of the day, as were Edward G. Robinson, Paul Muni, and Marlene Dietrich, a late Jewish arrival from Germany. Playwrights Lillian Hellman, Elmer Rice, and Clifford Odets were working on Broadway and in Hollywood. In Southern California, such major figures as the Warner Brothers, Samuel Goldwyn, Jesse Lasky, David Selznick, and Irving Thalberg dominated the production of the movies and built the great studios of Hollywood's Golden Age. By the mid-1930s the popular culture of the Eastern European Jews had become a basic part of all America's popular culture, and was no longer purely Jewish.

Louis D. Brandeis is shown here in 1919, three years after he was appointed the first Jew to serve on the United States Supreme Court.
(Library of Congress)

The move into the mainstream of American life went far beyond the popular arts. Louis D. Brandeis was the first Jew on the Supreme Court, in 1916. In the 1930s, Benjamin Cardozo and Felix Frankfurter were appointed to the Court. Joseph Pulitzer and Arthur Hays Sulzberger were two of the great newspaper owners of their times, Pulitzer at the *St. Louis Post-Dispatch* and *New York World* in the 19th century and Sulzberger in mid-20th century at the *New York Times*. It was Pulitzer who founded the renowned Columbia School of Journalism in New York and endowed the Pulitzer Prizes. The list of Jews emerging into and moving to the top of the American mainstream is very nearly endless. In classical music, American-born Yehudi Menuhin, Russian-born Jascha Heifetz, and Polish-born Arthur Rubinstein. In politics and government, New York Governor Herbert Lehman, Treasury Secretary Henry Morgenthau, and hundreds of others. In broadcasting, David Sarnoff and William S. Paley. In science, of course Albert Einstein, J. Robert Oppenheimer, and thousands of other distinguished trailblazers, researchers, and healers. At no time have people calling themselves Jews numbered as much as four percent of the population of the United States. Yet for a group so small, Jews have made an enormous impact on the life, art, and thought of the country.

For the Eastern European Jews of what was aptly called the Great Migration, the first step was often making a few dollars more than what was necessary just to survive. In the early years, those first few extra dollars went to bring the rest of the family over from Europe, and for such basic things as a little more food and a little better housing. By the mid-1920s, when the Golden Door was largely closed by discriminatory American immigration laws, there were a lot more dollars, a lot more being bought, and a lot of second-generation children—the children born in America—going to work for better pay. A great many of the Jewish immigrants and their children were still working in those years for relatively little, in some parts of the garment industry, as retail clerks, and in a score of other occupations. At the same time, the unions had brought better wages, many had gone into their own businesses, and new young professionals were beginning to come out of school and into the Jewish communities.

The 1920s were boom years, as well, years when all kinds of new machines and techniques were being introduced into the country. Automobiles were beginning to be mass-produced and bought by people

German-Jewish-American Joseph Pulitzer was called a "Leader of Liberal Republicanism" in this March 1872 cartoon from the St. Louis Puck. (Library of Congress)

of moderate income. For the first time, working people could buy such modern marvels as radios, washing machines, and record players. Housing was being built—not the crowded slum tenements of New York's Lower East Side, but whole new neighborhoods with wide streets and room to breathe. People began to go to the movies, to have the money to take vacations, to send their children to tuition-charging colleges in much larger numbers than the percentage of Jews in the American population, a trend that continues to this day.

Americanization

As all that happened, Americanization became the goal of most young second-generation American Jews. The old ways they thought to be hopelessly unsuitable for getting on in America. The old language, the old beliefs, the tight old Jewish communities—most young people saw all of these things as standing in the way of progress, and also downright embarrassing. This is not unique to Jews, being the main reaction of each second generation in the great majority of American ethnic groups.

One young second-generation Jew remembers riding on the subway with his mother:

> I remember, for example, we had relatives in Brooklyn. We used to take an elevator train, the Myrtle Avenue Line—oh, it took an awful long time to get from East 10th Street to Myrtle Avenue. And my mother would sit in the train and read a Yiddish newspaper—if she did, I would walk off into the next corner because I didn't want to be seen sitting next to conspicuously un-English-speaking and un-English-reading people . . .
>
> When I got to college and took education courses in the Education Department, there we had another problem because by that time the board of examiners of the Board of Education had developed the most refined ears in the world. They could detect not merely a Jewish accent, but that mysterious thing called the Jewish intonation. And so at City College we education students were continually being warned against the possibility of a Jewish intonation because that would flunk you on the orals. So there was a heavy premium put in the Public Speaking Department, the Education Department, all through the educational system, on ridding yourself of any possible remote trace

of a Yiddish speech pattern or speech habit.

This continual emphasis in the schools that you must not speak Yiddish, because it will affect your English speech and so on, made for gaps between children and parents. After all, I must have had some kind of uneasy relationship with my parents if I wouldn't sit in the same subway car with them while they were reading a Yiddish paper, you see. And so, the generational gap for immigrants was much different from that aroused for the native born, because there was a premium put upon being as different from your parents as you could, in speech pattern, in how you looked and how you dressed, and the kind of work you did, and so on. You had to get as far away from the old culture as you could.

You were told to forget, not to practice your old home language . . .

The English-only policy in the schools and in the culture of the time made for enormous family and personal strains—and for guilt that would last a lifetime. At the same time, it accomplished the kind of quick Americanization that Isaac Mayer Wise had successfully urged upon German Jews almost a century earlier. And in about the same amount of time, too.

The main story of immigrant Jews in America is one of tremendous progress, every step of the way. But not without struggle, heartbreak, and pain. For every department store tycoon, there were 10,000 poor Jews who worked their lives out in sweatshops so that their children could go to school. People did live in cold water flats, with neither heat nor air. All those young women and men did die in the Triangle Shirtwaist fire. And there was anti-Semitism—lots of it, and often from people you would expect to know better.

Anti-Semitism

In the 1920s, as large numbers of Jews moved out into the mainstream of American life, they encountered much anti-Semitism. Anti-Semitism was nothing new in American life, and as late as 1914, Leo Frank had been lynched after being convicted on a trumped-up murder charge in Atlanta, Georgia. But the move into the mainstream happened at the same time as a strong anti-foreign, anti-Black feeling developed in the country, and when such hate organizations as the Ku Klux Klan were growing rapidly.

Even as they and their children moved into the mainstream, many immigrants, like this small-town couple from Connecticut, continued to read newspapers in the language of the old country.
(Library of Congress, ca. 1940)

Young Jewish-American Leo Frank was lynched in Atlanta, Georgia, in 1914 after being arrested on a trumped-up murder charge. (Library of Congress, Bain Collection)

The most prominent and openly anti-Jewish bigot of the 1920s was Henry Ford, whose automobile company had also made him one of the richest men in America. In May 1920, his *Dearborn Independent* began to print a standard piece of anti-Semitic work, *The Protocols of the Elders of Zion*, which claimed to expose a Jewish plot to rule the world. The paper continued from then until 1927 to openly print a wide range of anti-Semitic articles and pamphlets. Ford was obsessed with his anti-Semitism, and would not change his course even though Presidents Wilson and Taft, heading a committee of 119 notables, asked him to do so. Nor did he give way to the public and private requests of many other individuals and church groups. Ford did finally apologize in 1927, when threatened with a million-dollar lawsuit and a boycott of his cars, but the apology was empty. He continued on his anti-Semitic ways until the late 1930s.

The other most notable anti-Semitic incident of the 1920s came from an entirely different source. This was the attempt in 1922 by President Lawrence Lowell of Harvard to openly establish quotas for the number of Jews to be admitted to Harvard. What was most notable about the event was that he tried to do so openly, for by then quotas aimed at limiting the number of Jewish students were common at most of the major private colleges in the country. Lowell eventually withdrew his open attempt, after a storm of protest, but that did little to change the underlying anti-Semitic situation in the colleges. Nor was anti-Semitism limited to Henry Ford, the Ku Klux Klan, and Harvard University. There was a widespread pattern of Jewish exclusion throughout the country. In banking and finance, industries often assumed to employ many Jews, the truth was just the opposite. There were a few "Jewish" firms on Wall Street, but very few Jews in senior jobs at the main American banks and securities firms. The truth is that Jews generally found it very difficult to secure professional and white-collar jobs throughout the 1920s and right into the 1930s.

Depression and War

The stock market crash of 1929 ushered in the Great Depression. With it, much changed for American Jews, along with all other Americans. Fascism had come to Italy in 1922; in the early 1930s, it came to Germany. With it came discrimination and eventually mass murder in Germany and throughout Europe, accompanied by a worldwide rise in anti-Semitism. In the United States, groups sympathetic to German and Italian fascism joined forces with homegrown anti-Jewish movements. However, the 1930s were also the years of Franklin Roosevelt and his New Deal, which brought to power people with strong drives toward democracy and against bigotry. In the Roosevelt years anti-Semitism in America became no longer respectable—even when it was whispered over a white table cloth in an exclusive club, rather than shouted by a bigot wearing that white tablecloth, as a Ku Klux Klan hooded robe.

One of the best known American bigots of the 1930s was Charles E. Coughlin, a Catholic priest. He did a national pro-Fascist, anti-Semitic radio program that attracted many listeners. He also ran a newspaper, *Social Justice*, which reprinted the *Protocols of the Elders of Zion*, thereby performing much the same role in the 1930s as Henry Ford had in the 1920s. His work and views were not endorsed by the Catholic Church of the time—but that Church made no attempt to stop him.

The two most effective fascist street organizers in the United States at that time were Joe McWilliams and Fritz Kuhn. Their aim was to organize street-fighting organizations, like those of Hitler and Mussolini, preparatory to a Fascist takeover in the United States. Their main weapon was to try to stir up hate—against Jews, Blacks, foreign-born Americans, Socialists, Communists, anarchists, labor unions, the New Deal, and anyone else they found useful to hate. McWilliams organized the Christian Front, trying to develop a very broad organization that would appeal to every kind of hater. Kuhn organized the German-American Bund, meant to appeal to German-Americans sympathizing with Hitler and the Nazis. Both had limited success, but the tide of the times was against them. As the 1930s wore on, and Hitler became more and more despised by Americans, it became harder to push anti-Semitic views. There were exceptions, as in New York's heavily German-American Yorkville neighborhood, but even there Kuhn's Bund was always a small, although noisy, minority force. Similarly, McWilliams' Christian Front found fertile ground for anti-Semitism in some of New York's poor Catholic neighborhoods, but was nowhere a dominant force.

For American Jews, such people as Coughlin, Kuhn, and McWilliams were a major worry. But their main economic concern, as it was for all Americans, was how to survive the Depression. Most did, and far better

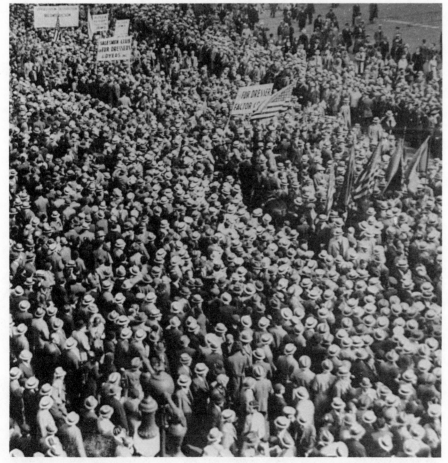

As the full horror of the Nazi atrocities became clear, people like these 40,000 in New York City in 1944 called urgently for help to save as many Jews as possible.
(National Archives)

Along with religious items for sale, this New York City store proclaims in 1942 that "It's great to be an American."
(Library of Congress)

than many people of other recently arrived ethnic groups. Although many were unemployed and many had businesses that went bankrupt, there were also highly skilled workers, business people, and young college graduates and professionals in the American Jewish communities.

Their main social and political concerns had to do with social legislation in the United States and the rise of fascism abroad, especially with its growing threat of genocide—mass murder—of the Jews in Europe.

After the early 1930s, when Franklin Roosevelt and his Democratic Party were firmly in power, the overwhelming majority of American Jews became Roosevelt supporters and across-the-board Democratic voters. Even the Socialist *Forward* supported Roosevelt in the 1936 presidential election and from then on, becoming in many ways far more liberal than Socialist. In the mid-1930s, and until the Nazi-Soviet Pact of 1939, even the American Communist Party supported Roosevelt. After that Pact, the Communist Party became isolationist until the Nazis invaded the Soviet Union. Many Americans, including many Jews, had supported the Communists as being consistently against Hitler. Now most turned against the Communists and stayed against them.

But supporting the New Deal may also have contributed to the greatest failure of the New Deal and of the American Jewish community in the 1930s. For, even while knowing what Hitler was and what the Nazis were doing to the Jews in Germany, the New Deal and the American Jewish community failed to reopen the Golden Door in the 1930s, this time to the hundreds of thousands of Jews and other refugees who would have flooded in from Germany and then from other European countries annexed by Germany before the Second World War. Some intellectuals and prominent Jews were allowed to come to the United States—perhaps 25,000 in all—but the great mass of Jewish refugees was left to die in Europe. Albert Einstein came; but for every Albert Einstein tens of thousands of Jews who could have come to America died in German concentration camps. There were all kinds of reasons at the time: disunity in the American Jewish community, the need to unite Americans for the greater battle to come against fascism, not having full knowledge of what Hitler was doing. But the net result of not opening the door to refugees was the unnecessary death of hundreds of thousands of European Jews.

December 7, 1941, marked a real turning point, for American Jews, as for all other Americans. From then on, and for four very long years, the whole world was at war, and fighting and winning that war was the major

Irving Berlin sang "Oh How I Hate to Get Up in the Morning," in his own show, This Is the Army, *but his most famous song is probably "God Bless America."* (Copyright *Washington Post*; reprinted with permission of the D.C. Public Library)

concern of each day. There were battles over discrimination against Jews in the armed forces, and also large-scale development of win-the-war activities among Jewish organizations. And substantial agitation began for the development of a Jewish state in Palestine. Zionism had gained strength in the 1930s, as the fate of the Jews of Europe became clear. The failure of the United States, Great Britain, and other Western democracies to come to the aid of the Jews was obvious to Jews all over the world. Many Jews began to feel that their only real hope was to help themselves by forming a Jewish state in Palestine.

9

The Jewish-American Heritage in Our Time

By the end of World War II, much had changed. At home, the Depression was over, and America was entering what would turn out to be a quarter-century of prosperity and growth, ending with the boom of the 1960s. There would be recessions, but nothing like the Great Depression that was such a bitter recent memory to tens of millions of Americans. There were homes to build and enjoy, children to raise and send off to school, new cars to buy, and all the other good things that can come with a victorious peace.

Abroad, Hitler and Mussolini were dead. They had murdered six million Jews in what is rightly called a holocaust, and many millions of others, as well. American Jews were no longer fighting for the life of their country, or quite literally for their own lives. They could and did return to the pursuits of peace. At the same time, most felt that there was unfinished business, in the form of a homeland for those small remnants of the European Jewish community that had survived the Nazi mass murders.

By the beginning of the postwar period, some very basic things had changed for the American Jewish community. For one thing, there were far fewer poor Jews than before the war. After the war, American Jews were more and more middle class, in income and in where and how they lived. Many still continued to work in the garment trades and other occupations as blue-collar workers, but even these tended to be rather well-paid skilled workers. Some poor American Jews still worked at low-paying jobs, but far fewer than at any time since the turn of the century.

One of the most famous Jewish immigrants of modern times was Albert Einstein, the great physicist and humanitarian who fled Nazi Germany in the 1930s and became an American citizen in 1940.
(Library of Congress)

Roughly half a million new Jewish immigrants came to America in the decades after World War II. They came from Europe after the war, including Eastern Europe and the Soviet Union. Later, some came from Israel. Even later, tens of thousands of Russian Jewish immigrants came to America, in those periods when the Soviet government was willing to let some of them leave. Many of these new postwar Jewish immigrants were poor at the start, and began the process of adaptation to a new world by learning English and taking whatever jobs they could get.

Pockets of poverty could still be found in some of the old ethnic neighborhoods, especially among those who were beginning to retire without adequate retirement incomes. Later, similar pockets of poverty developed in such places as Miami Beach, where many retired people found that small retirement incomes and high inflation had destroyed their savings.

Yet the great majority of American Jews all during the modern period have earned enough to adopt middle-class lives, whatever their occupations. By the 1980s, almost half described themselves as professionals, somewhat less as managers and businesspeople, and less than one-tenth as laborers.

Moving Out to the Suburbs

That being so, most American Jews were also making enough money to join the huge American move to the suburbs after the war, a move that continues today. All over the country, large numbers of Jews settled in what often became largely Jewish suburbs, such as Great Neck, Lawrence, Scarsdale, Skokie, Levittown, and scores of others. Some of the more affluent suburbs, like Great Neck, were often called "golden ghettos." But, of course, they were not ghettos—no one forced Jews to live there. People lived in these suburbs as a matter of choice, clustering with people of similar backgrounds. As the mass move continued, many of the old Jewish city neighborhoods changed greatly, first holding far fewer Jews and then very nearly disappearing. But not all, for in some cases new immigrants and new Jewish groups moved in to fill the areas. That is why Brighton Beach, in Brooklyn, is as much a Russian Jewish community—though much smaller—as was the Lower East Side at the turn of the century. That is also why there are large communities of ultra-

Orthodox Jews in several New York City and nearby suburban areas. Also, Jews in these decades have moved out all across the country, far beyond the cities and their suburbs.

Some rather easily predictable things happened in the Jewish suburbs—and some rather unexpected things, too. On the predictable side, most of the old Socialist, Communist, and Anarchist ideas lost a great deal of their force and following. The Jewish-Socialist or Communist of the 1930s usually found it easy to become a suburban liberal in the 1950s and 1960s.

Also rather predictable was the flight of many young, college-educated people from any kind of Judaism. That was and is a major trend, as young people marry those of other faiths, or for any other set of reasons move away from religion altogether. The trend is a cause of enormous concern for Jewish religious and ethnic leaders, just as it was for Portuguese-Spanish and German-Jewish Americans in their time.

Religious Revival

What was rather unexpected was that so many suburban Jews would move toward Jewish community life and toward Judaism, rather than away. Several reasons for that mass move have been advanced, none of them entirely satisfactory. For many it has been as simple as a search for personal roots, a common pursuit for second- and third-generation people in many American ethnic groups. For a great number of Jews, it is also a real need to identify themselves to those who are not Jewish. This is a simple, clean way to avoid even the slightest chance that someone may think they are running away from their Jewishness because of possible anti-Semitism. After Hitler and the war they fought against him, most American Jews were not at all inclined to deny their Jewish roots. This was so even for many Jews who were not believers or active in Jewish community affairs.

In the suburbs, there were also the children. "What am I, Mommy?" is a question that has to be answered, no matter how uncertain or uneasy is the answerer. In the new suburbs, Reform temples and Conservative synagogues flourished. So did Sunday schools and Saturday schools and youth clubs and community centers. Actually, the temple or synagogue itself often became the Jewish community center, with appropriate addi-

Actress Marlene Dietrich (here shown in The Blue Angel) *left Germany for Hollywood before Hitler and his anti-Jewish policies took full hold.*
(Copyright *Washington Post*; reprinted by permission of the D.C. Public Library)

Jewish-American Herbert H. Lehman was director general of United Nations relief efforts during and after World War II. (U.S. Office of War Information, Library of Congress)

tional buildings on nearby land. Nor was it all that difficult for the new Jewish suburbanites to take this path, for many adults wanted a community-centered life, too. As to the religious aspects—well, many a suburban rabbi has privately deplored the religious level of his or her congregation, while rejoicing at the level of its activity and support. It has been that way before in America. Many a Lower East Side Socialist sent children to Orthodox synagogues, for basically the same reason.

There has also been a considerable religious revival among American Jews, especially in the 1970s and 1980s. The ultra-Orthodox Hasidic movement has grown, and in the process attracted thousands of young American Jews. The Orthodox branch of Judaism has in recent times grown, as well, as have both Conservative and Reform Judaism. In all, about 3,000,000 people are affiliated to some sort of Jewish congregation (out of about 5,500,000 American Jews).

The Impact of Israel

The presence of the state of Israel has also provided a focus for, and developed considerable national pride among, many American Jews. Between the end of the war in 1945 and the establishment of Israel in 1948, American Jews were heavily involved in convincing the American government to support the formation of Israel. Since then, American Jews have had much impact upon the survival and development of Israel. They have exerted great pro-Israeli influence upon the American government and raised enormous amounts of money for Israel. Thousands of American Jews have also immigrated to Israel, before and after the establishment of Israel as a nation. Zionism had not been a large influence in the United States before the 1930s, but with Hitler's rise to power and the attack on Europe's Jews, it began to gain strength. By the time World War II had ended, it was a strong force in American Jewish life, and gained great strength between 1945 and 1948, as Israelis struggled to establish their new nation. After the war, some American Jews worked on the ships smuggling Jews from Europe to what was then Palestine. American Jews were active in Israel's fighting forces, and American Socialist-Zionist Jews settled in the Israeli cooperative communities, called *kibbutzes*. Very religious American Jews, nonbelieving American

Jews, and everyone in between was involved in that fight, for the idea of a national homeland proved to be tremendously powerful after the 1930s and the war.

One American Jewish immigrant, Golda Meir, became prime minister of Israel, from 1969 to 1974. Born in Kiev, Russia, in 1898, she immigrated with her family to the United States when she was eight years old. She grew up in Milwaukee, Wisconsin, went to school, married, and became a Zionist in the United States. Then in 1921, she and her husband immigrated to Palestine, where they stayed for the rest of their lives.

Not all of the American Jews who went to live in Israel have stayed. Many have returned to the United States, for a wide variety of reasons. Some have spoken of differences in living standards, lack of professional opportunities, and the fact that Israel has been at war with its neighbors ever since 1948. Others have simply found out that they wanted to continue to be Americans, rather than become Israelis. Whatever the reasons, the return flow from Israel has been considerable. There has also been a considerable Israeli immigration to the United States, composed of people born in Israel, and of people born elsewhere who have lived in Israel for some time.

The existence of Israel, and its long war with its neighbors, has had a powerful impact upon Jewish-Americans. For decades now, the support of Israel has been a major project for many American Jewish organizations, though some ultra-Orthodox groups have disagreed for a wide variety of other reasons over the decades. Israel's existence and long war have been a focus and rallying point for large numbers of American Jews, and are probably in part responsible for the revival of American Jewish religious and community feeling in our time. When Israel's war is done, much may change in the American Jewish community and world.

In the modern period, organized anti-Semitism has lessened. It has not disappeared, though. There are still bitterly anti-Semitic radical-Right hate groups in the United States, though on a much smaller scale than the Christian Front and the Bund of the 1930s. For a little while, in the late 1960s and early 1970s, there were also moderately successful anti-Semitic leaders in some portions of the Black community. Some of these remain, but their influence is small. And there were still, as late as the mid-1980s, some private clubs that excluded Jews from membership, although there are even more that exclude Blacks and members of other discriminated-against ethnic groups.

Moving On

American Jews continue to merge and mix with all other Americans, carrying their history and heritage into the larger American community. Today, so many American Jews are doing so many notable things in so many ways that just listing them would take a book much longer than this one. Novelist Saul Bellow, scientist Jonas Salk, playwright Arthur Miller, historian Barbara Tuchman, violinist Isaac Stern, singer Barbra Streisand, Olympic swimmer Mark Spitz, industrialist Irving S. Shapiro, merchant Stanley Marcus, philosopher Elie Wiesel, singer-composer Bob Dylan, actor Dustin Hoffman, coach Red Auerbach,

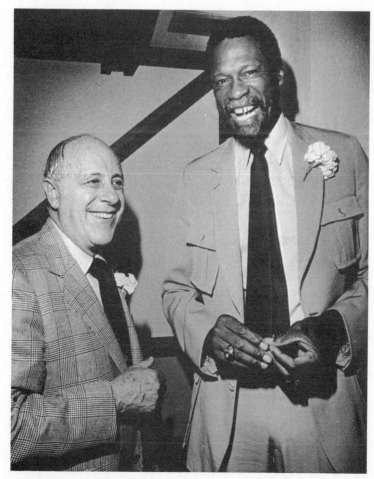

Jewish-American Red Auerbach changed the game of basketball, with Bill Russell and the other players of the Boston Celtics. (Copyright *Washington Post*; reprinted with permission of the D.C. Public Library)

actress Lauren Bacall, conductor Leonard Bernstein, poet Allen Ginsberg, hair stylist Vidal Sassoon, architect Louis Kahn—thousands of American Jews are making major contributions to the nation and the world. And it continues. With each generation, the Jewish-American contribution to the whole of American society grows.

Suggestions for Further Reading

Antin, Mary. *The Promised Land*. Cambridge, Massachusetts: Houghton Mifflin, 1912.

Baum, Charlotte, Paula Hyman, and Sonya Michel. *The Jewish Woman in America*. New York: Dial, 1976.

Birmingham, Stephen. *Our Crowd: The Great Jewish Families of New York*. New York: Harper and Row, 1967.

————. *The Rest of Us*. Boston: Little, Brown, 1984.

Brownstone, David M., Irene M. Franck, and Douglass L. Brownstone. *Island of Hope, Island of Tears*. New York: Viking Penguin, 1986.

Cowen, Philip. *Memories of an American Jew*. New York: Arno, 1976; reprint of 1932 edition.

Feingold, Henry L. *Zion in America*. Boston: Twayne, 1974.

Glazer, Nathan. *American Judaism*. Chicago: University of Chicago, 1972.

Handlin, Oscar. *Adventure in Freedom*. New York: McGraw-Hill, 1954.

Howe, Irving. *World of Our Fathers*. New York: Simon and Schuster, 1976.

Howe, Irving, and Kenneth Libo. *How We Lived: A Documentary History of Immigrant Jews in America*. New York: Richard Marek, 1979.

Karp, Abraham J. *Haven and Home: A History of the Jews in America*. New York: Schocken, 1985.

Libo, Kenneth, and Irving Howe. *We Lived There Too*. New York: St. Martin's, 1984.

Liebman, Arthur. *Jews and the Left*. New York: John Wiley, 1979.

Marcus, Jacob Rader. *Early American Jewry*. Philadelphia: Jewish Publication Society of America; Vol. 1, 1951; Vol. 2, 1953.

Meltzer, Milton. *The Jewish Americans: A History in Their Own Words, 1650-1950*. New York: Crowell, 1982.

————. *Taking Root: Jewish Immigrants in America*. New York: Dell, 1976.

————. World of Our Fathers: The Jews of Eastern Europe. New York: Dell, 1974.

Metzker, Isaac. *A Bintel Brief*. New York: Ballantine, 1971.

Miller, Wayne Charles. *A Comprehensive Bibliography for the Study of American Minorities*, in two vols. New York: New York University, 1976.

Novotny, Ann. *Strangers at the Door*. Riverside, Connecticut: Chatham, 1971.

Roth, Cecil. *History of the Jews*. New York: Schocken, 1961.

Sachar, Abram Leon. *A History of the Jews*. New York: Knopf, 1968.

Sachar, Howard Morley. *The Course of Modern Jewish History*. New York: Dell, 1977.

Sanders, Ronald. *The Downtown Jews: Portrait of an Immigrant Generation*. New York: Harper and Row, 1969.

Schappes, Morris U. *A Documentary History of the Jews in the United States*. New York: Schocken, 1971.

Schoener, Allon. *The American Jewish Album: 1654 to the Present*. New York: Rizzoli, 1983.

Thernstrom, Stephan, ed. *Harvard Encyclopedia of American Ethnic Groups*. Cambridge, Massachusetts: Harvard University Press (Belknap), 1980.

Wertheimer, Barbara Mayer. *We Were There: The Story of Working Women in America*. New York: Pantheon, 1977.

Wischnitzer, Mark. *To Dwell in Safety*. Philadelphia: Jewish Publication Society of America, 1948.

Index